HITTAZ

Get It Back In Blood

LOU GARDEN PRICE, SR

URBAN AINT DEAD PRESENTS

CONTENTS

Submission Guidelines   vii

Acknowledgments   ix

Introduction   xiii

Chapter 1   1

Chapter 2   9

Chapter 3   17

Chapter 4   31

Chapter 5   37

Chapter 6   43

Chapter 7   53

Chapter 8   59

Chapter 9   65

Chapter 10   73

Chapter 11   81

Chapter 12   91

Chapter 13   99

Chapter 14   107

Chapter 15   111

Chapter 16   119

Chapter 17   121

Chapter 18   125

Chapter 19   127

Chapter 20   133

Chapter 21   139

Chapter 22   147

Chapter 23   155

Chapter 24   161

Chapter 25   167

Other Books By   175

Coming Soon   177

Books by URBAN AINT DEAD's C.E.O   179

URBAN AINT DEAD

P.O Box 960780

Riverdale GA., 30296

Cover Design: Angel Bearfield / Dynasty Cover Me

Edited & Interior Design: Khloe Cain / Khloe's Thoughts Editing
www.khloesthoughtsediting.com

Contact Author at: paralegal.louprice@gmail.com (for book editing, ghostwriting quotes).

Snail mail: LOU GARDEN PRICE SBI 00454309

Delaware DOC 1101

PO Box 96777

Las Vegas Nevada 89193

**See: GettingOut.com/create account

Search Lou Garden Price SBI #00454309

James T Vaughn Correctional Center, Smyrna DELAWARE

For tablet connection. Download the gettingout.com app.

Contact Publisher at www.urbanaintdead.com

Email: urbanaintdead@gmail.com

Print ISBN: 978-1-7355238-6-6

Ebook ISBN: 978-1-7355238-7-3

SUBMISSION GUIDELINES

Submit the first three chapters of your completed manuscript to urbanaintdead@gmail.com, subject line: Your book's title. The manuscript must be in a .doc file and sent as an attachment. The document should be in Times New Roman, double-spaced and in size 12 font. Also, provide your synopsis and full contact information. If sending multiple submissions, they must each be in a separate email.

Have a story but no way to submit it electronically? You can still submit to URBAN AINT DEAD. Send in the first three chapters, written or typed, of your completed manuscript to:

URBAN AINT DEAD
P.O Box 960780
Riverdale GA., 30296
DO NOT send original manuscript. Must be a duplicate.
Provide your synopsis and a cover letter containing your full
contact information
Thanks for considering URBAN AINT DEAD.

ACKNOWLEDGMENTS

First, thank God.

The whole gang at URBAN AINT DEAD, LLC. Including Elijah R. Frecman, CEO/AUTHOR & Publisher. Shout to all the UAD authors, especially those I've worked with: Eliza Paige Williams, Derrick Rollins, and the whole line up.

To all my sister, Prissy, who has held me down from the cradle and her husband Chad for your unwavering friendship. (See: Bradburymassage.com).

My comrade Kwame "Dutch" Teague. You know it's all real live love from this side, homie. Good looking out on the Foreword and plugging Elijah in at BET. And to ya wife, and my sister, Jay René, all the same. Can't have one without the other. Shout out to PRISONRIOTRADIO.COM. Prisoners everywhere need to get up on it and for anyone ain't see the DUTCH movie on BET.com need to check that out.

To my West Coast comrades: incarcerated publishing boss Mike Enemigo and Janet Key at The Cellblock. (THECELLBLOCK-.NET). And all of those down with us and what we're doing. Such as Guru, Silk, Suge Knight and everyone else. Shout out to all y'all out there.

Selena Panasik, I thank God for giving me a true friend this past 27 years. I been in this bitch 21 years and look around and see very few who stuck by me through thick and thin. Love you shortcakes. #mymiracleinthebronx1996. (Lena5789@gmail.com).

Janell Price, Lil Lou, Mykela I love all of you until my very last Heartbeat. Hold y'all head out there. To Sherain a.k.a Raindrop, Laverne and all The Fonder family, thank you for looking out for my children in my absence.

Xiania Sonnét—I will always love you, LC, my love and prayers are with you, Lee, Layanna, and all of yours.

Can't close this out without saying something about all the love being shown to my last novel, the blockbuster SOSAFROMSCAR-FACE: The Saga Begins! The latest reviews are 4.2 out of 5 Stars on Amazon. THANK YOU! THANK YOU! THANK YOU

For all the support to all my readers.

Good looking out Jake. Love you for everything, kid! To anyone I missed, my bad. I should be catching up to you next time because there's many more coming!:-)

ONE LOVE IT'S THE BROOKLYN WAY!
LOU GARDEN PRICE, SR.

For Xiaa Lou Garden Price, Jr. who was taken from us way to early (1999 – 2021).

INTRODUCTION

Kwame "Dutch" Teague

There are a few writers in this game that not only have crazy skills, but are the type of stand up dudes that I fuck with the long way. Lou Garden Price, Sr. is one of those dudes. I reached out to Lou several years ago when I saw his book being advertised in a magazine. The book was set up like a sequel to Scarface and I thought it was a genius idea. Lou is a thinker, a planner, a strategist and an all around solid dude. Lou, you've kept it 1000 since we met, opening the door to mutual opportunities and sharing your network unselfishly. I salute you comrade and I'm glad to see you finally getting your chance to shine. To the readers out there, the book you are about to read is one that I feel is destined for the silver screen because it has it all: a good pace, a good story and a fire ending that will have you tweaking for more. What more can I say? The urban game has been oversaturated with mediocre stories that seem to be telling the same story over and over, so trust and believe Hittaz is that fire!!! So without further adieu, I give you Hittaz...

CHAPTER ONE

(The Villa Strip club*East New York*BKNY*Monday 12:00 AM)

Joker Red was what everyone called him, but his government name was David Leon Hodges. He was a light-skinned black man, thirty-one years of age, with green eyes and powerfully built. He had a single gold tooth and wavy hair; the women loved him at first glance. He sat quietly in the rear left backseat of the sleek new 2020 Buick Century as his first cousin and business partner Skeeter Dukes weaved in and out of the late evening traffic on Atlantic Avenue near Brooklyn's Fort Green Section.

Skeeter passed a lit blunt of purple haze to their closest comrade, Ghostman Dinero, who sat shotgun.

"You good, Red?" Black N9NE, who was seated behind Ghostman, inquired. "How's it feel to be outta the joint?"

Joker acknowledged him with a slow nod. "Exhilarating."

The four men had been close since pissy pampers in childhood and all of them were a part of a crew called "EVERYTHING IS EVERYTHING" or EIE—a Brooklyn gang they'd started back when they were still in middle school. Now they were all in their 20s and 30s, with Joker being the eldest at thirty-one, and the only one of the four who had been to prison.

EIE had been through hell together. They had fought in the military together - - where they'd lost comrades together, yet one amongst them had betrayed Joker to the pigs. The entire time he spent on the inside, he'd breathed hatred and vowed vengeance against the Judas who'd sold him down the river for thirty pieces of silver.

They were members of a highly organized stick-up crew that robbed and killed drug bosses, and on most occasions, they hit banks. Because robbing and kidnapping drug kingpins was so profitable, EIE had set up their own lucrative drug dealing network in Brooklyn, to sell the stolen merch. Four years ago, however, Joker had been caught after he had just firebombed a jacked SUV that had been used in a bank hold-up earlier that day. He was able to burn all the bank robbery evidence, including the disguise he had worn, along with the gas-saturated car, so the armed robbery charges could not stand without physical evidence linking him to the crime scene—especially when the state's best witness had failed to identify any of the EIE members in a police lineup. Therefore, Joker had escaped his most serious charges and had to be given a plea bargain on the arson and grand theft auto charges, which was a slap in the face to prosecutors and the police. Subsequently, he was sentenced to 0 to 4 years in state prison.

Now, he was free. And to celebrate his release, his entire crew were headed to the Villa Strip club in East New York to get their party on.

Skeeter turned down the Rick Ross club banger and looked into the rearview mirror at Joker. "Since you were doing time up north, I expanded the crew."

Joker glanced behind them. "I see the five car fleet."

"Yeah."

"Nice cars," Joker commented. "You always liked the flash. I hate it. The prisons are filled with niggas who like flash. You know what they do now?"

Skeeter sighed sarcastically. "No, but you'll tell me."

2

"They are all broke. They call home on expensive phone calls to broke black families, begging for ten and twenty dollar money orders. The fuckin' flash gets the attention of the law, who never see you going to a job. They know, because you tell 'em, that you doin' crime when you roll down the street in a hundred thousand dollars in vehicles."

Skeeter didn't want to argue. "They're basic cars."

Joker stared behind them once again.

A Ford Expedition.

A Buick LeSabre.

A Honda Accord.

A Nissan Pathfinder.

And the Buick Century.

Each of them were last year's editions. All black.

In Joker's view, the fleet was anything but basic.

"Most of them we know from Fort Green," Skeeter explained as they stopped at a red light on Rockaway Avenue and Livonia Avenue in Brownsville. "Others we know from school and the military. All are hittaz, killaz, stickup men and plain ole miscreants. Wolves thrown back like fish in the sea by Uncle Sam, with nothing but horrifying memories of war and atrocities from over there. You remember Baghdad, Kandahar, Lybia, battles with Al Qaeda, ISIL and others?"

"Can't forget it," Joker recalled. "Especially the *others.*"

The warriors in the car were quiet, somber, at Joker's words. They were all haunted by the same memories.

"I figure it like this," Ghostman said as they rolled down New Lots Avenue and into East New York, turning left onto Pennsylvania Avenue. "We were over there killin' people with skin the same color as ours, and they were poorer than we could ever be. So, I may as well come home and kill some no good black mufuckas who sell dope that ain't poor."

"Makes sense to me," Black N9NE added.

They turned another left onto Livonia and parked in front of

3

the Villa. Skeeter climbed out of the car and stretched as he adjusted his Gucci glasses on his brown-skinned face. Every member of EIE eventually surrounded the Buick Century and dapped each other.

While the sinister crew scanned the faces of each person in the crowd, Joker's eyes were busy studying the faces of the twenty-two-man squadron, carefully and calculatedly. Skeeter had been correct; most of the men were familiar comrades. There was, of course, Joker's brother Big Al; Khadafi who was Skeeter's cousin and right hand; there was Fly, Jeff Lightfoot, Boo, Knarf, Blaze, Hard Knox, Bonecrusher, Broliks, Fast Eddie, Big Chief, Monk, Mustafa, Ground War, A-Son, Divine The God and one face Joker was not familiar with...

"Who is he?" Joker asked Skeeter.

"I'm Meth Man Ace," the tall man answered after overhearing Joker's inquiry. "I was stationed at the Tenth Mountain Division, New York. I live in Atlantic Terminal."

"So I guess crystal meth is your specialty," Joker stated conversationally.

Ace nodded. "I can make a few more chemicals than meth, sir."

"Joker Red," he reminded him. "Call them whites 'sir,' not me."

"It's a big crew," Joker observed in earshot of Skeeter.

"Yep," Skeeter nodded. "And I'm runnin' it just fine, cuz."

Joker smiled at him. "Chill, duke. No need to get your panties in a bunch. You da man now. You run it."

"Damned good to see you home, Red!" Fast Eddie greeted him, shoving a thick bankroll into Joker's hand. The two old war comrades embraced.

Joker looked down at the money, and his face lit up. "You still any good at safecrackin', E?"

"Hence the name," Eddie returned. "The boys and me took up a small collection for you. Anything else you need, lemme know, baby."

"That's right, comrade," Joker nodded, appreciating the love. "Let's go on in and see some bitches."

———

A City Girls hit was banging up in the club, causing all the strippers to go buck wild.

They partied like they were rich when they were really just getting by. The "licks" were not lining up like they needed them to and some EIE members were becoming desperate. They had kids to feed, let alone themselves. In any event, tonight was a special night because of Red's release, and Skeeter meant to enjoy it. The City Girls song was followed by Da Baby's best hit as the EIE crew entered the main floor area.

The club shook with a feel good vibration. The twenty-two-man team was led upstairs by a honey-skinned redheaded goddess dressed in revealing pink plastic boy shorts that were riding high up into her thick derriere. She motioned for them to follow her upstairs to VIP, where they were obviously expected.

"Dayyyuuummmmmmm!" Ghostman exclaimed as her thick down south butt cheeks bounced up the stairs. The men could actually see the moist, dark pussy lips underneath the pink plastic crotch covering. "WOW. That's all I gotta say...wow."

She only smiled at the effect her body had on them as they all craned their necks to stare at her magnificence.

"Fuck, baby doll," Skeeter said into her ear as she passed out VIP passes to all of them. "Please tell me you're stayin' up here?"

"I'll be in and out, big guy," she promised, noticing Joker Red— the silent one. "I'm Uzenna Jade, your VIP hostess."

Girls were all over the place. Quality seating aligned the walls and floor areas. The booths were either small or large, decorated with opaque golden curtains that could be pulled closed for privacy. Tables had been spread out around the stage area for smaller groups of club goers yet the crew chose the large party booths to sit in. It wasn't long before the club's top female dancers converged on EIE.

"Who's the guest of honor?" asked a white girl named Brittani Dane. She reminded Joker Red of one of those stacked white girls inside Kream Magazine.

"Why, hello," she whispered as she sat next to Joker.

Joker, aloof, nodded her way. "Hey, beautiful."

"Should we go to a private room?"

"Nah, baby, just dance and do ya thang," Joker instructed her as the buckets of Ace of Spades came out. "Drink with me. That's all you gotta do."

For the next hour, they all had fun with the dozens of nude and near nude strippers. Uzenna Jade never did come to dance, and Joker didn't think she would either. She was obviously the club's most beautiful girl, making her its number one. She was a unique and special standout, so Joker had to summon her over to a private booth and close the curtains.

"You're not from New York, huh?" he pointed out.

"No. Mississippi," she informed him.

"A dangerously beautiful southern import," he commented.

She appreciated the compliment. "Thank you," she said as he covered her with his black leather blazer jacket.

"This may sound corny," he started. "But are you already spoken for?"

She suddenly stood up. "I need to get back to work."

Joker also got to his feet. "Hold up, baby. Just lemme say...I think you're different from all the others. I know I am. I'm a different breed altogether."

She opened up the curtains to the booth and paused. "I'm a long and complicated story."

She left his blazer in the chair and scurried off, leaving him even more intrigued about her. Joker, feeling the effects of the alcohol, went back out on the floor to see his crew heavily engrossed with the strippers in VIP. He caught a fleeting sight of Skeeter heading towards the bathroom.

Joker decided to follow him. When he walked in, Skeeter was down on his knees in the first stall, vomiting his guts out.

"Aw, shit," Skeeter puked out loudly. "Damn!"

"You aight, cuz?" Joker asked, concerned.

"It's just the gin, homie," Skeeter breathed, his face still hovering over the toilet as the nausea hit him again.

"Ayo, my man," Joker whispered in his ear. "I know what you did."

"Wha—?" Skeeter turned to look up at Joker, but it was too late. The straight razor appeared from nowhere, swiftly slicing a deep red canal across Skeeter's throat from ear to ear. Blood spurted and sprayed from the jugular vein.

Skeeter tried to scream as he clutched his throat but instead fell backward onto the toilet seat, wide-eyed with fear as he convulsed. He stared up at his cousin, shocked.

"Why?!"

"You filthy rat bastard," Joker hissed at him with a cold, vengeful smile. "You put the jakes on me when I went to firebomb the getaway car. You were the only one that knew the spot I'd picked out to burn it! You made a grave mistake, cuz. You sent detectives. No way detectives would just happen upon an arson. I spent four years waitin' to kill you."

Before Skeeter could reply, he lost consciousness and bled out.

Once Joker was sure Skeeter was dead, he hoisted his body so that he sat up on the toilet seat and locked the stall. Then he leaped over to the neighboring stall wall and cleaned his hands in the sink. He used brown paper towels to wipe the walls of the stalls clean of fingerprints and wiped the blood off the floor as best as he could. He flushed the straight razor and the paper towels down the toilet before slipping out of the bathroom to rejoin the party.

Welcome home, Joker Red.

CHAPTER TWO

(Uzenna Jade*Queens,NY*Monday Morning)

The club was closing, and it was not until then that EIE members grew curious that their leader, Skeeter Dukes, was unaccounted for. By this time, however, they were all pretty inebriated, ready to head home for the day. In fact, that's exactly what four of the other car loads did; they rolled out.

Joker stayed frosty the whole time. He never flinched.

"He probably left with some bitch," Ghostman offered with a tired yawn. "He a grown ass man, we ain't waitin' for his black ass. I'm drunk, tired, and got this young bitch waitin' at the crib to suck my dick before I go to sleep…. let's ride."

"Plus, he got the fuckin' keys to the car," Black N9NE reminded them. "I'm callin' Uber."

The Uber took ten minutes to get there, and as the men were making their way in, Joker hesitated.

"Y'all go ahead," he told Ghostman and N9NE. "I'ma call my own uber if he don't show up."

"Aight, Red," Ghostman said, embracing him. "We'll get up, Playboy."

"Aight then, big homie," N9NE told him. "See ya at HQ later."

9

"Most def." Joker waved at them.

Once they were gone, Joker Red looked around and walked down the street towards Pennsylvania Avenue. He was all the way up near New Lots Avenue when a horn honked from a cash green Lexus. He was about to ignore the occupants when he noticed Uzenna Jade in the back seat.

"Need a ride, daddyo?" she offered from her rear window in her sensual down south drawl.

"Daddyo?" one of the girls inside the car whispered.

"Yeah, nosy bitch," Uzenna snapped at her. "I'm choosin' this nigga so shut the fuck up and mind yo business."

They must notta found the body, he thought to himself. "Hell yeah, baby girl. Is there room in there?" he asked as he looked into the car's interior.

"Yep, c'mon," Uzenna told him as she opened the door. "We're headed out to Jamaica, Queens. Where you tryna be?"

He climbed into the backseat, next to the honey-colored beauty. Up front sat two other stunning dancers: Coral Nee aka White China, who was a very light skinned Chinese girl of 19 years old. She drove the 2019 Lexus. In the passenger seat, next to her, sat the Alexis Texas lookalike, Brittani Dane.

"Where you want me to be?" Joker asked her in return.

Uzenna visibly inhaled while looking him over. Her pussy throbbed with attraction for him, but there was more to it than that.

"You ain't nothin' but trouble, huh?" she teased.

"Uh huh. And you ain't?"

"Hey, Britt. Y'all bitches hungry?"

"Starving," Brittani answered. "We met, remember, sexy?"

Joker nodded. "How can I forget?"

"In case you did, I'm Brittani Dane." Brittani pointed to Coral. "That's our China doll sister Coral...we call her White China cuz she so fuckin white!"

"Fuck you, slut," Coral giggled, buzzed from drinking all night.

"Joker Red, at your service," he introduced himself.

Coral took Linden Boulevard into Queens and stopped at the 24-hour IHOP on Pennsylvania Avenue. They were all famished. Once they were finished eating, Joker Red took Uzenna by the hand and kissed her inner wrist. He led her to a private booth where they sipped on mugs of hot herbal tea.

"How many men have offered you a better hustle?" Joker asked, choosing his words carefully. "A better life?"

She laughed sarcastically. "You mean Villa men?"

He nodded. "Indeed."

She shrugged nonchalantly, looking bored with it. "Well... hundreds, maybe even a thousand. And you say you're somehow different?"

"Don't doubt it," he stated smoothly. "I'm a man of my word. I'm a devastatingly real mufucka. And I move calculatedly, so what I'm thinkin' won't be revealed until I know enough about you. See, you think because you are a beautiful goddess, with the pussy to match, that that's what I want. It's not. Everybody else does. That's why I'm different."

She brushed a hand through her soft red bushy hair, and her light brown eyes pierced into his soul. "You are so sexy," she sighed.

He loved her long, thick, red hair and how the tresses hung loose all around her face.

"You, too, baby," he responded. "I need more from you than sex, though, as hard as that may be to imagine right now. Cuz...I think we both wanna go somewhere and fuck each other's brains out this very second."

She felt her nipples harden and her pussy moisten at his words.

"Oh, yeah," she managed to squeak out.

"No man? No chains?" he asked her.

"I can't just up and leave." She looked away, connecting eyes with her girls. "I have others I need to be concerned about."

He was silent, compassionate, and attentive. "Are you bein' forced to do what you do? What am I missin' here?"

She hesitated furtively, but nodded. Then, in a low voice—almost a whisper—she told him all he needed to know. "You'll get me killed, my sisters killed, my closest girls, and them. She pointed at Coral and Brittani. We could be bein' watched right now."

He saw the fear in her eyes.

"Okay, okay...shhhh," he soothed her. "Be easy, baby."

"Uzenna, let's go!" Coral pressed her.

On their return to the the Lexus, Uzenna told Coral to drive them home on Queens Boulevard. Once there, Brittani and Coral went in while leaving the car running with Uzenna and Joker inside.

"So, this is where you live, huh?" Joker asked while committing the house to memory.

"This is it," she told him.

The house was a large four-family dwelling with no driveway but it had a large porch area.

"Twelve of us stay here," she explained. "I'll be real with you because I do want out. We work for the Italian-owned Eccentric Models, a front company for sex trafficking. It's bigger than me, than us. I want to walk, no, to run, but...what about my sisters? There are three of us, plus the other ten girls. We're all a family."

"Nothin' is impossible, Uzenna," Joker said calmly. "You are caught up in a matrix. The good thing is, I know my guys aren't afraid of anything. All ex-military. What if we came into the Villa and killed all them greaseball cocksuckers?"

"Well, I did see your impressive looking crew, so I can see y'all doin' that....but you have my belly flippin' out. You guys have done things like this before, huh?"

He waved nonchalantly. "Killin' is nothin'. How many of them bastards are we talkin'?"

"I think fifteen," she guessed. "That's just here in New York. There's other Mafia connected with them in New Orleans and Mississippi."

"Can we catch these all in one spot?"

"I, um..."

She was unsure. Uzenna was just another innocent doe-eyed young girl caught up in the crossfire, trying to weave her way through the wicked whims of men. Joker obtained her cellphone number and saved it in his phone.

"I'll get an Uber to take me home." He took a minute to use the Uber app before looking at her again. "Lemme ask you something, doll baby—let's just say this....If I had a hustle—an illegal but highly profitable, revolutionary scheme—where I needed girls, and that hustle didn't include them having to have sex...but will lace y'all's own pockets...how many girls can you get?"

"Thirteen from the door," she confidently answered. "It won't be the easiest sell to them becuz it's an unknown to them. I have to have more information."

Joker thought for a moment. "Drug smugglin'. Small quantities. A lot of small quantities."

"On us or inside of us?"

Perhaps she wasn't so innocent after all. "Both."

"And you're sayin' you need all thirteen of us?"

"Yeah."

She trailed off, searching for the right words as the sun rose. Queens Boulevard was coming to life with the morning rush hour traffic.

"We've been lied to and manipulated for sex for too long now," she stated with a stone-faced expression. "Now you come sayin' no sex. Plus, we all eat? Most importantly, we stay together... and we can walk if we wish?"

"No chains, no threats, no sex, freer than birds," he swore. "I need some badass bossy bitches, with a Queen like you to lead them. They'll be kept safe. I'll pay all overhead. You can say no anytime, and it'll be honored. It's not my style, desire, or intent to pimp or enslave women. I'm tryna scheme after millions of dollars, and if I have a team of pretty bitches on my side—bitches with felony in y'all heart—I know I'm on my way."

He paused to spark up a blunt of purple haze.

"Let's be real," he spoke as he exhaled a big plume of smoke. "It's the mob I'ma have to go up against. That ain't no fuckin cakewalk. If we go through all that...a war in the streets...then it has to benefit me way more than y'all's sex can ever sell. What I been plannin' is gonna take us all the way to the top."

She felt it in her gut that she should trust him and ride with him. "You plan whatever you want. If it breaks me and my girls free from Mafia hold...that's all I care about. If it's successful...we'll owe you a large debt of loyalty."

He nodded. "You understand what I'm sayin' here?"

"What am I, some naïve stupid bitch?" she said with a smile. "I get it. People are gonna die."

"Right."

He stared into her eyes for a moment.

"You need me to trust you," she added. "Well, you need to trust me, too. We just met...this is all gut reaction right now. And what I think is a mutual need."

"And mutual respect," he told her.

"And extreme attraction."

She made him smile with that last comment.

She returned the smile.

"The minute I saw you, I knew you were the piece of me that had been missin'," he admitted with deep sincerity. "Like the universe put us on each other's paths on purpose."

"You sure are somethin'," she commented, feeling a sense of admiration for him. "Who are you? Where have you been all my life?"

"Told you I was different," he boasted. "I'm a different breed, cut from a different cloth. Truth is, I'm a gangster like you never seen or heard of. And that's *gangster* wit the 'e-r' at the end. Not the 's-t-a' like these gay punk mufuckas in skinny jeans runnin' the rap game and the streets. I'm a bank robber and militant killa that won't hesitate to put a nigga or bitch, dick or titties in the dirt if crossed."

"I believe it, and I like it." She exhaled smoke from the blunt as she talked. "You found a boss chick when you found me. I'm not dumb, but I'm a young girl willin' to learn if you wanna teach me."

A brief moment passed when they held hands and he kissed her lightly on her soft lips.

"Somethin' big was born last night, and today," she observed.

"It damned sure was," he agreed. "And I'll teach you everything."

His Uber ride arrived.

He exited the Lexus, stalling when Uzenna got out of the Lexus and stood in front of him.

"Okay...so what do I do? Where do I start, daddy?"

"Don't worry," he assured her, pulling her close to him. "I already started it. Later today, shit will hit the fan at the Villa, and y'all won't have to work. Follow my lead, and if anyone ever asks you...I'm just a trick that really digs you. I'm harmless."

More like Amerikkka's nightmare.

Then he was gone.

CHAPTER THREE

(Fort Green*Brooklyn, NY*Tuesday, 4:22 PM)

Skeeter's sister, O'Mira Dukes answered the door for the two White female veteran NYPD detectives the evening after employees at the Villa had discovered the body of Skeeter Dukes. By this time, Skeeter's entire family was present at O'Mira's Fort Green apartment.

"I'm Detective Sergeant Jacquelyn Pope," the blond forty-something-year-old cop made the somber introductions. "And this is my partner, Detective Hanna Genovese."

O'Mira, still in tears after hearing the news from police earlier in the day, led the two detectives into a packed living room and kitchen area. All told, there were about fifty people that were present in the project apartment.

"I see that everybody's here, huh?" Sergeant Pope stated compassionately. "We are terribly sorry to meet you all like this. This was a senseless act, and we were sent to investigate and bring justice to whoever did this. I'm so very, very, very sorry for everyone's loss..."

"Thank you," Skeeter's mother, Minnie Dukes, said.

"OK, slowly now..." Pope continued as she turned on a small digital recorder. "Your exact address is what?"

"Thirty three Navy-walk," Minnie told her. "Apartment 4-A, Brooklyn, New York..."

Skeeter's twenty-two-man crew were there, and most were unwilling to speak to the NYPD, let alone admit to being at the scene of the crime.

"Everybody knows y'all was at the club last night!" Minnie scolded them. "Khadafi...Al...Joker..."

"Aunt Minnie," Al spoke up. "Nobody trusts pigs. Especially not the NYPD who kill niggas for fun. Look at what's poppin' off in the streets around the world! Eric Garner, George Floyd, the race riots, Tamir Rice, Michael Brown, Fernando Castile, Sandra Bland, the prison food strikes, the James T. Vaughn prison riot in Delaware, the Black Lives Matter protests and the international movement. Niggas is tired everywhere. Cops are our mortal enemy. We talk to these bitch pigs, and they'll make us suspects anytime they want to twist up the narrative of Skeeter's death."

"We're just trying to do our jobs," Hanna calmly said. "We're sorry for your loss and are extremely regretful for the despicable act of murder upon George Floyd, Eric Garner, and so many others in this country. But your family member was heinously murdered via Colombian necktie in the stinkin' strip club bathroom. Please forgive me for bein' blunt, but someone in that club knows something."

"Was there a fight?" Pope asked. "Among your group, with bouncers perhaps? Did Skeeter—"

Joker's voice interjected from across the room, "The Villa is owned by the Mafia."

"The Mafia?" repeated Pope. "The New York Mafia?"

"Collaboratively," Joker explained carefully. "New Orleans, and at least one of the five New York crime families."

"And you know this how?" Genovese inquired.

"Lady," Joker laughed cynically. "Word on these Brooklyn streets is that the Villa is into sex traffickin victims across state lines. Maybe Skeeter was getting too close."

Pope and Genovese glanced at each other. "Your name, sir?" Pope asked.

"Forget my name," Joker waved her off. "This is info that's too sensitive to put citizen's names on. Or I'll be killed next. If y'all were up on your homework, you'd already known about the human traffickin' network from the FBI or your Major Crimes Unit."

"You're in a room full of men who fought for the individual freedom of every U.S. citizen," Ghostman added. "We stopped true bad guys in the Middle East from kidnappin' and enslavin' thousands of girls...so we know how to recognize the stink of men like them in our own back yard. And you don't?"

Big Al looked at the detectives. "Why are you here? Way over here in Fort Green? Is NYPD takin' Mafioso money to look the other way while young girls are bein' forced into slavery and God knows what else?"

"Now we're the suspects?" Pope asked, irritated.

"You damned right you are!" Eddie snapped.

"Y'all bitches gotta go," Khadafi advised the two detectives. "Ain't no love here...get the fuck out."

The two officers exited the apartment quickly.

"The Villa is Mob owned?" Big Al sounded surprised.

"That's the word I got," Joker answered.

"The Italians run it," Blaze elaborated. "But who cares? They run a lot of businesses in the empire."

"What? Who cares?" Ghostman shot back. "We care! A nigga cut a smile in the big homie's neck! The God gotta be avenged!"

That sentiment rippled amongst the group.

If they only knew what that rat fuck did to me, Joker thought as he sat in silence.

"Okay, then," Ghostman sighed. "What's the plan? We ridin', we raidin', we robbin' them greaseheads or what?"

Method Man Ace smiled to himself as he looked across the

room at Joker Red. Ace thought, *son had something to do with it. This is no coincidence. Joker comes home, and on the same night his cuz is necktied? You gots to be one cold-blooded mufucka to pull that shit off. Lemme see how all this shit plays out. It should be interesting.*

"Joker Red?" Black N9NE glanced over at him. "Looks like you're back up. We followed your cousin's leadership while you were in the pen. He gone now...and EIE is really yours, right?"

"Let's respect Auntie and O'Mira's house for one," Joker stood up. "The temperatures are flarin' right now. We bury our comrade in a week, and we'll meet at EIE HQ for the after party. There, we'll discuss eatin' those greaseheads for breakfast. I'll have a plan of attack by then."

Little did they know, Joker already had one.

———

"Hey, O?" Joker approached her inside her bedroom. She was not much of a looker, but she had a kind disposition about herself. He gently hugged her. "You gonna be okay, cuz?"

She nodded sadly. "Why'd they have to kill my brother like that? Slit his throat like a sheep, though?"

Joker sat at the foot of the bed. "I don't know, but I need everything he has that you stashed for him. The money...guns, credit cards, checks, everything."

She never even blinked. "C'mon, all this illegal shit he had goin'...If Mama saw the weapons, she'd freak."

He loved the sound of that. All he had to his name was the cash Fast Eddie had given him from the collection, which was almost $2000. O'Mira led Joker into Skeeter's bedroom and opened the door with a security lock key. His room was expensively decked out and immaculately maintained.

"What I'ma do wit all of it?" she said, exasperated. She opened up the closet, turned on the overhead light, then pulled out a milk crate and lift the bed sheet down inside of it. "Guns, bullets... take 'em all. There's a lot more he keeps in the EIE offices."

"Aw, yeah," he proudly nodded. She gave him the keys the police had given to her. "They gave you his personal shit already?"

"His wallet, everything," she said. "All them cars are EIE, Inc., property that's in my name now. I'll sign it all over to you, Red, cuz I can't have that Mafia shit at my doorstep. I'm scared for my kids. Move it all out."

"I'll take care of all the bills," he promised. "I'll handle it."

There were two nine millimeters, a pair of twin Glock .45s, a rocket launcher, a machine gun with an RPG attached, several riot guns, and Desert Eagles, an impressive arsenal, to say the least. O'Mira opened up a cash box stashed inside the floor safe and removed a stack of money, jewelry, credit cards and a checkbook. *There's a bank account for EIE, Inc.*, he thought to himself. *Good, the nigga was witty, looks like $14Ks in there... Is that it? 14 fuckin K?*

Joker counted the cash in there. "It's only four grand here. The $14k in the account is for the business. We need at least twelve g's to send him off right."

"I'll leave you to figure it out." She exited the room.

Joker used Skeeter's credit cards to pay for his own funeral arrangements. Bushwick-Aberdeen Funeral Home was quick to say the credit cards were good to cover a "fine home going for Mr. Dukes."

Joker maxed out $20,000 on Skeeter's cards, being sure to transfer $5000 of it into his own bank account while he was at it. After he'd made all of the arrangements, he packed up everything he wanted to keep of Skeeter's in suitcases and green army duffel bags.

"Hey, cuz," Joker said to O'Mira before leaving. "I handled everything and left you written notes. Flowers, limos, times, dates, everything. I need to follow up on other stuff. Look here...give some of this money to Auntie. It's only fifteen hundred but lemme put the rest of it to work, and I'll be back to take care of y'all."

He hugged her and Minnie before exiting.

That evening, close to 11:00 PM, out of curiosity, he took an Uber out to the Villa nightclub. As he'd suspected, the club was silent, except for about ten to fifteen of the staff being present. Joker pulled out his cellphone.

"Hello," a sweet southern voice answered.

"Red here."

"Oh my gosh," she squealed happily. "This is Uzenna."

"I know that pretty voice anywhere," he flirted.

"I was hopin' you'd call."

"Can we meet up?"

"Now?"

"Yeah." He gave her directions to the Ramada Inn near JFK Airport. "I already sent and paid an Uber for you."

"I'm on my way."

It's time to put the clutches on this fine ass Mississippi bitch, Joker thought.

————

He opened the car door for the honey-colored southern doll as she stepped out. She was dressed in a cute blue jean Burberry dress and a Prada sweater. They hugged warmly and walked inside the hotel. Joker's room was on the sixth floor. Once inside, he took her sweater off and closed his eyes as he inhaled her Chanel No. 5 fragrance.

When she saw the dreamy look on his face, she giggled. "You like me?"

"Can you tell?"

He hung the sweater over the cushioned chair she sat on.

"Lemme get right down to it, mama." He turned up the heat and sat across from her on the bed. "Will bein' out cause trouble for you?"

"Not as long as I bring money back," she said shyly.

"Don't trip," he assured her. "We have to play their game for now....is three hondos cool?"

"Three hundred?"

He nodded and handed her three one hundred dollar bills.

"That's more than fine." She put the cash away.

"I lead that crew you saw," he began. "We normally take down high value targets like drug bosses, banks, armored trucks, and cash checkin' spots, but you should know that I just finished doin' four years for arson and grand theft auto for fire bombin' the stolen getaway car after a robbery."

She held a hand up, eager to say what was on her mind. "A body was found at the Villa."

He paused. "And?"

"You told me..." she hesitated. "Later today, shit will hit the fan at the Villa..."

"Okay...and what?"

"Well, a fuckin body was found, and we all had to be questioned by the pigs," she reported with a shrug. "They showed us photos of his dead ass. I mean, we knew nothin', saw nothin'....did you...?"

"You know nothin', saw nothin', heard nothin', right?"

She nodded. "Sorry."

He continued. "I need you to trust me. You're a sex traffickin' victim, and I'm plannin' to take Amerikkka by storm. I need women to help me do it. Women that won't snitch. And I need a bomb bitch like you to help me recruit other bitches. I'm no pimp. I love women. I love pussy. I love everything about females. I love them too much to see a top notch, class A, superior bitch like you get dogged out by dirtbag tricks. Together, me and you are gonna shut them bastards down and send them to hell. Take a look at what I got here."

He retrieved the suitcase and duffel bag full of weapons. He opened them and pulled out one of the rocket launchers.

"Lemme introduce you to my little friend!" he said, using the famous movie quote.

"Oh my gosh," she whispered like a little girl. "I seen one of those in *man on fire*."

Standing beside her, he caught another whiff of her sweet feminine scent. "You recall who Denzel Washington saved in that movie?"

"A little girl," she told him. "A kidnapped little girl."

"Ain't that kinda like you?" he stated, hardening against her soft buttcheeks. "You need me to free you?"

She turned to look up at him, and she saw the pent up years of hunger in his pretty green eyes. He wanted her...needed her...but it wouldn't be right. He pulled away.

"Forgive me," he said to her.

"No reason to."

She kissed him and placed his hand on her jutting left breast. "Lemme take care of you...and that super hard dick tryna bust outta your pants..."

She led him to the bed, and he tongue kissed her lips. She tasted like butterscotch. The way he kissed her had her feeling like he was a ravenous pussy eater. She absolutely loved having her coochie and ass eaten and hoped he would. He undressed her down to her sexy white lace panties. She wore no bra, which gave him a nice view of the loveliest breasts he'd ever seen. He sat down and put his face against her soft belly as she stood in front of him.

He stared up at her with his green eyes. "You smell good... I can tell from right here your pussy smells like mango."

He pulled her panties tightly up into her seam and inhaled her juicy hot crevice. She shivered in his arms as he grabbed her big, Mississippi, deep south ass cheeks. He stripped her naked and put her onto her back underneath the covers. He toyed with her red hair and looked into her innocent doe eyes.

"I never seen this before," he murmured to her.

"What's that, daddy?"

"Sweet girlish innocence," he said sincerely. "Like a cute Catholic schoolgirl on one side and on the other, a cold-blooded wicked bitch whose pussy is drenched at the thought of sleepin' with a real gangster."

"Oh, god, yes," she moaned as he sucked on her nipples. "I'm so wet, it feels like I peed."

Damn! He thought.

He removed his boxers and her mouth gaped open when she saw his long, thick member. *He has a fuckin porno king dick*, she thought. A girl didn't get that all the time! She was nervous.

"I don't think I can fit you inside me," she shook her head doubtfully.

"You makin' me your daddy, right?"

She nodded and touched him. "It's enormous!"

He laid her on her back. "You gotta trust me. Lemme be your daddy, and you be my little mommie."

He went down on her and was surprised that her pubes were also reddish-brown. "You are a true redhead!"

He inhaled her sweet young pussy and began to lick, nibble and kiss her from clitoris to anus. She tasted delicious. She moaned, and her juices squirted as she climaxed and humped slowly onto his mouth.

"God, I love this pussy!" he murmured and gulped as he drank down her syrupy fluids. "Mmm, so gooodd!"

He tongued her clitoris again and built her back up to another orgasm.

"Oh my god, I'm cuming," she screamed as her body shook with pleasure. "So fuckin good." She propped herself up and looked at him with a seductive smile. "You like that yummy squirtin' girl cream, huh daddy?"

"Fuck yeah!" He couldn't take it anymore.

He climbed towards her face, and she knew exactly what to do with his enlarged shaft. She soaked the stalk with her spit, from the head to his balls, licking and spreading the wetness with her tongue and lips.

"I can't wait," he gasped.

He climbed on top of her and began sliding the large plum-sized head of his inside her. She was leaking wet like a faucet. She took him halfway like a champion, and that was all he needed. Whimpering and crying out from the initial pain, he knew he had to stay still and allow her to adjust to him. She felt like a virgin, he thought as they tongue kissed and started to fuck.

"Oooh yes," she moaned, "you're splitting me wide open around this big dick!"

As a sheen of perspiration broke out all over her honey-colored body, he became acutely aware of how good she really did smell as a woman. She reached down and grabbed ahold of his buttocks to guide him as he maintained his slow pace. He was mindful of his huge size and was careful not to harm her lovely little thick nineteen-year-old body.

"Oh, shit," she whispered. "Fuck me!"

"Damn, girl!" he moaned. Being inside such Grade A, tight pussy after four years of having no sex was mind blowing. "Your pussy is so good, mommie!"

They started going at it as he kept his strokes long and steady until he lost control. She squirted her milky liquid nectar all over his cock and balls.

",YYYEEEESSSSSSSSSSSSSS   BAAAAAABBBBYYYYYY GIRL!!" he grunted as he came hard. He felt himself blasting her insides with gushers of warm thick cum. "Uzenna....."

"Uhhhmmm, cum in me...so good, daddy," she moaned in his ear. She shivered under his sweaty body and sucked along his neck and throat. Her vagina clenched at his still deeply buried shaft. "Been so long since I felt a man's cum in me....I needed that."

"I shouldn't have taken advantage."

"What? It was the most beautiful thing I've ever felt! I never squirted with a man inside me. Only with masturbation or a female's tongue."

"Oh, yeah?" That made him feel good.

She climbed on top of him.

"On everything I love," she swore. "There's a connection between us that's insane. I let down my guard with you. We needed each other tonight."

She got emotional all of a sudden, and tears flowed from her pretty light brown eyes.

"Hey, you straight now," he assured her. "I bet high on the underdogs. And that's what we all are. Every dog has its day...and this is our fuckin' day."

"I hate dancin'," she revealed. "I despise strippin' naked. First, it was my father touchin' me and my sisters. We ran away and started workin' in this off-book casino in Jackson, Mississippi. They said we owed all this money for housin' us and feedin' us. That's how they get you. They don't chain us. They killed and beat boys and girls in front of us, so we were too afraid to run. They also raped us and drugged those who were a problem. They also keep cops on payroll."

"How'd you end up in New York?"

"We were sold," she told him. "The boat burned, and there was all this talk in the apartment we shared wit twenty girls. Thirteen of us were driven up here in a van. I think the others were killed because they were strung out on heroin. If you get hooked, too fat, ugly, unsaleable, they'll kill you and feed you to pigs and gators."

"Real fuckin gators?"

"Yep, they chop you up," she quipped. "I was forced to watch a friend die, get chopped up, and fed to gators. They used me to spread fear into the group because of what I witnessed. It got so depressing...I was thinkin' of suicide only a week ago. Until I met you."

"Yeah, well..." he looked at her. "No way, mommie, forget about it. That's exactly why I wanted to lay off sex from you. You been through enough abuse."

"It wasn't abuse, daddy," she reminded him. "I call you daddy because I really choose you. Just take care of me like I never been taken care of. You're my John Creasy, like 'Man On Fire.' You comin' to rescue me."

His eyes got misty when she said that. John Creasy was the character portrayed by Denzel Washington in the epic movie 'Man On Fire'. Dakota Blue Fanning played the little girl who had been kidnapped in Mexico. She had called Denzel her "Creasy Bear" out of love and loneliness. In the end, John Creasy had traded his life for her freedom. 'Man On Fire' happened to be Joker's favorite Denzel movie.

"I hope to be half the man that John Creasy was," he expressed to her. "You'll see it's all love and loyalty with me."

"We created somethin' special tonight," she swore to him. "Awww, man...now you got tears in your eyes?"

She dried them and kissed him.

"I told myself in prison," he began, "that all I need is one good one. Just one...older, younger, don't matter. And with her...we'll burn Amerikkka down from beneath the ground where no one can see it."

"Okay, Riddler. Whatchu mean exactly?"

"Prisons." He rubbed her back and dried her eyes. "Amerikkka has five percent of the earth's population, and twenty-five percent of the earth's prison population. It's a capitalist/colonialist black and Latino slave business, no doubt. What I saw in there were men in pain. Wantin' freedom is pain. Wantin' to hug loved ones is pain. Wantin' sex with ya woman is pain. And there is only one pain reliever in prison."

"Drugs?"

"Yep." He nodded. "When I was in there, them niggas turned me on to K-2. A synthetic weed that's hard to detect in a regular urine test. They use all kinds of shit in there. Tramadol, Neurontin, Lyrica, etcetera. But they want real shit, and I aim to provide it."

"What's the plan?"

He smiled. "To move a massive flow of odorless, colorless, residue-free, undetectable narcotics right into every major prison mailroom in the United States. And those COs will deliver the shit directly to our sellers for immense profits."

They made love again and did not fall asleep until 5 AM.

CHAPTER FOUR

(The Villa*Brooklyn, NY*Wednesday 12:07 AM)

"What are you so fuckin' giddy about?" Fat Tony asked Uzenna as she passed by, smiling, on her way up to VIP. It had been nine days after the bathroom murder. Fat Tony, the boss of the Brooklyn outfit, couldn't help but stare at her beautiful tattooed ass cheeks and the way they swallowed up the white G-string she wore. He liked Uzenna. "Godamnit! How do you keep your ass lookin' so thick like that?"

"Huh, Tony?"

"Just get your ass in my office....*now.*"

She frowned but complied.

Minutes later, Fat Tony was plunging his big fat body behind Uzenna as he fucked her unwilling pussy with his short greasy penis. She yelled and moaned fake pleasure as he quickly grunted and ejaculated into the condom he wore. He gave her a crumpled up twenty-dollar bill and sent her back to work just as the telephone on his desk started to ring.

"The Villa," he growled into the phone, breathless.

"Hey, Fat Tony!" the thick Italian accent boomed from the other side of the line. "It's Sally."

"Salvatore! Whattaya say ya bum?"

"Ya hear we comin to town, huh?"

"Beautiful news!" Fat Tony said. "I hear ya nephew Max is getting made."

"Yeah, yeah. We need your place to do it," Sally told him. "Any problems wit that?"

"Don't insult me. Of course it's okay. Fuhgeddaboudit! Done. Anything you say."

"Fantastic," Salvatore replied. "You'll be ready, security and all, Saturday then?"

"We'll have it all perfect on Saturday."

"Beautiful, " Sally said. "We'll reimburse you when we get there."

"Fuhgeddaboudit. See you then."

Fat Tony hung up and noticed Uzenna still in his office, pulling her thong up into her ass crack, which he couldn't help staring at.

"Whaddaya still here for, like we're married or sumptin'" he yelled at her. "Get your pretty ass out there and make my fuckin money!"

Now she had something to really smile about.

———

(EIE HQ*4:25 AM)

Uzenna knew she had to be careful because one wrong move could get her killed. So, she waited until the club closed and had Joker send her a Lyft car to bring her out to Fort Green at EIE HQ. The driver took Uzenna to Fulton & Willoughby and let her out in front of EIE Headquarters.

When she stepped out of the flashy Lincoln Navigator, she saw a large group of men on the corner shooting Cee-Lo, drinking beer, and smoking kush. The fact that it was 4:25 AM never seemed to bother them. One of EIE's black fleet cars banged a hit record by NBA Young Boy.

EIE Headquarters was a pool hall on the second floor, six large apartments on the third floor, and the Jamaican Sun Restaurant on the ground floor. Around the corner, on the Willoughby side, was a basement apartment where the EIE's narcotics were being sold from.

"Damn, babe!" one of the young thugs said as Uzenna walked past them. "Can I have some fries with that shake?"

"Ay, stupid!" Joker barked from the window upstairs. "Respect the fuckin' first lady! Come on up, Queen, Uzenna. Don't worry about my lil niggas."

"First Lady?" the thug whispered once Joker was out of earshot. "More like *'First Phat Ass'* I seen all night!"

The surrounding young niggas snickered, and the one who cracked the joke stooped down and rolled the dice.

Uzenna climbed the stairs to the pool hall, where she saw Joker and ran into his arms. "Hey, daddy, we need to talk. In private. Now!" she demanded.

He ushered her into his office, and she immediately began telling him all she had heard about the upcoming Mafia Omerta ceremony that was going to be secretly held at the Villa on Saturday.

"That's big time news," he said.

"That's why I ran over here," she reasoned.

He sat next to her on the sofa.

"Tell me about this Salvatore Bonanno," he probed. "And where does he fit on the chess board."

"He's the king," she proclaimed. "Don Salvatore is the big boss. He's based in N'awlins, across the Mississippi Delta, all throughout Mississippi."

"He's the head of the snake."

"Exactly."

"Hm." Joker rubbed his hands together. "You have serious homework to do. You are my only insider. So, you have to make sure there are no girls in the club when we hit it."

"None will be," she stated confidently. "We ain't allowed nowhere near there durin' ceremonies. Made men only, and they're strict about it."

"I bet." Joker bit his bottom lip. "We gonna hit it...and I mean hit it big like...this will be like hittin' the Pope. Once them rockets and grenades start flyin' through them doors and windows, it's over. You understand that, right? It's war with the Mafia."

"It'll be justice," she nodded.

"I call it righteousness," he countered.

"Well...I'll settle for righteousness. It'll all be the same to me."

Tears stung his eyes at hearing that.

"Yeah." She recalled the rape she had to endure the night before. "I'm angry, too....I sure would love to watch them burn."

He stared at her. "Too risky. After the rocket attacks, bullets will start to fly. My men will street sweep the whole place, and you can be struck."

Silence.

"Today is Wednesday," he told her. "We only have three days to plan this out. You have to get the girls packed up and relocated here."

"Here?" she repeated.

"There are empty apartments in this buildin'," he informed her. "I own it. You'll be safe until we move to my new base, where we'll launch the prison plan. I'll bring y'all with me wherever that'll be. You'll have to abandon your old identities, vehicles, cellphones, bills, social media... everything they can track you through. Follow me?"

"Yep. I'm so nervous. This shit done got so real."

He placed a hand on her knee and squeezed it. "Don't be nervous. Feel free and be liberated. In the wars we fought in, this is exactly the type of shit we put our lives on the line for. So them bastard extremists can never enslave Amerikkkan women...and look. You're bein' enslaved by our fuckin own countrymen."

She hugged him tightly and started to say something but stopped herself.

He knew she'd open up eventually without him having to ask. Such as the gator story. *I'm no one's judge*, he often thought to himself. *I'm a nightmare gangster. 'Man on Fire.' Her John Creasy.* He felt fortunate to have found this beautiful honey rose. This goddess. *She doesn't willingly sell pussy... She's bein' raped every day of her life by these mafia mufuckas, and we about to put a stop to it.*

"Daddy?"

"Yeah, Butterfly?"

She grinned all giddily at him suddenly. "Why you call me that?" she asked.

"Because that's what you are." He smiled at her kittenish charm. "Your almost child-like innocence. You are so beautiful, like ...the Monarch Butterfly caught up in the spider's web. And all you needed was someone to come along and untangle those lovely wings of yours and set you free. You're a goddess. You have no business being forced into shit. But don't worry, we about to boss up."

"You're gonna make me cry."

"No more tears. Just vengeance and liberation."

"The romantic killer."

"For you," he kissed her, "I'll kill anyone who gets in your way. You ready for a nigga like me? I ain't *nuttin* like you seen before."

"I'm not just ready for you, I'm destined for you," she declared.

He just nodded.

"Why they call you Joker when you clearly are no joke?"

"Because when I kill a mufucka, I smile," he said, giving her a demonstration of his sinister smile

.

———

(EIE HQ*Brooklyn, NY*Wednesday 5:30 AM)

"Family only for this one," Joker ordered Ghostman.

"You're EIE's underboss, so I'll leave it up to you to put this operation together," Joker looked him in the eyes. "There won't be any payout in this job, but it's critically important to the big picture of EIE and our bottom line."

"Aw, yeah, nigga..." Ghostman grinned, exposing a mouthful of gold and diamond teeth. "Army Rangers mufucka. Syria style."

"Rangers, nigga," Joker nodded and dapped his comrade. "ENERGETICALLY I WILL MEET THE ENEMIES OF MY COUNTRY..." he quoted part of the Rangers Creed. "Bashar Al-Assad all day. Rockets like BK have never seen to destroy those sex trafficking terrorists."

"I like it. Is that it?"

"Let's get to it."

CHAPTER FIVE

(EIE HQ* Brooklyn, NY*Thursday 12:00 PM)

Joker steered clear of the deadly mission he had Ghostman putting into motion. Unlike Skeeter, Joker did not trust twenty-two men to keep their mouths shut about something so massive, especially with the kind of heat it would bring. There was little doubt that all the major authorities would be alerted about the attack. ATF, FBI, and HSA would be all over a hit like this. Even Joe Biden would be at least briefed about it.

Joker got to his next order of business and sent for Meth Man Ace to come up to EIE HQ's the next afternoon. When the tall, light-skinned, twenty-nine year old entered the office, he shook Joker's hand.

"Okay," Meth Man Ace laughed nervously. "What I do wrong?"

"You're the one EIE member I don't really know, but at this point, I'm most interested in knowing." Joker sat behind the desk eating a hot curry goat and rice meal from the Jamaican Sun restaurant downstairs. "Sit and break bread with me, comrade."

"Good lookin', son," Meth Man Ace gratefully replied as he removed an aluminum dinner plate from the plastic bag it was in. "Still hot, too. Thanks, boss."

"You got it, baby," Joker told him. "You're a drug chemist."

"I studied pharmaceutical science," he informed Joker. "After wasting three years as a combat medic in Kandahar, I came home to nothin'. So, I started makin' small quantities of methamphetamines and mastered it. It paid the bills."

"Paid or pays?"

"Both."

"Is meth all you make?"

"Meth is my specialty, but I can manufacture a few things."

Joker had an idea already in mind. He pushed his laptop across the desk and turned the screen towards Ace. It was a list of drugs he intended to work with.:

•Heroin

•Methamphetamine

•Acid

•Oxycodone

•Oxycontin

•Tramadol(Ultram)

•Vicodin

•Welbutrin

•Molly

•Fentanyl

•K2 Liquid

•Percoset

•THC

•Suboxone

•Methadone

•Neurontin

•Lyrica Meth Man Ace was tearing into the jerk chicken and rice meal while inspecting the list at the same time. "Okay..."

Joker nodded and explained. "What on that list can you manufacture?"

"Fentanyl, meth, acid hits, K2 liquid, and molly," he listed. "I mean, technically, I could counterfeit 'em all, but if we shootin' for highest profits, those would be my top five."

"Top quality."

"If the ingredients are top quality, we can be millionaires," Meth Man said.

Joker stood up and stared out the window. "Most of the fiends are white folks in the suburbs and Wall Street now. The niggas and Latino niggas have been plucked off the streets and put in prisons. The white niggas are bein' catered to with thousands of Recovery Centers of Amerikkka commercials, Addiction Network hotlines they can call, and much more. The poorest Blacks and Latinos are uninsured. Whites go to rehab when they get arrested, but niggas are imprisoned. Why, when OBAMACARE was signed into legislation by a black president? We can't afford rehab, and the system is run by racist prosecutors and judges who are more likely to lock us up than them crackers. Anyway...I need you to create a shitload of drugs for me."

"Clarify shitload."

Joker turned to him and handed him a package of greeting cards. "To start, I want these saturated in colorless, odorless, K2 liquid, meth, molly and acid. I plan to flood Amerikkka's prisons with paper product narcotics. Thereare cats out there who know what time it is, like SPICE4FUN.com. They sell the ready-made K2 paper for $500 for two sheets, and lookin' at it with the naked eye, you can't tell shit. "

"What about the prison mailroom cops?" Ace asked.

Joker shook his head no. "Not even with a black light. Like if you just haphazardly spray meth or K2 on paper, they can use a black light to bust that shit comin' in. No, not us. Your job is to figure out ways around the black light tests, naked eye searches, and dog sniffing. We need a massive production of all those paper products for national distro."

"I can get it done, my nigga," Meth promised. "Youse a genius, son."

"Focus on the massive stockpiles, and I'll focus on the mass distro system. Be organized, be safe, and most of all, be secretive."

"I don't do no talkin'—" Ace began.

"Anh-anh," Joker put a finger up to his lips. "Just don't do it!" he warned, then paused for a full ten seconds.

"Sit here in the office and write out a plan," Joker pointed to the desktop computer. "You don't have an endless budget. Start with eight grand, spend it wisely."

Joker also gave him $500 for himself.

"Thanks, boss"

———

(The Villa*Thursday 12:45 PM)

"You gotta think they'll have tight security," Black N9NE whispered as he and Ghostman conducted recon on the Villa from Pennsylvania Avenue in a silver Dodge van with tinted windows as they used binoculars to spy on the club.

"No doubt," Ghostman replied. He picked up the two-way radio. "Silver Lightning to Blue Streak live, over."

Down at the end of Livonia Avenue was a dark blue Chevy van that held Big Al and Khadafi. "Blue Streak live, over," Al replied.

"We got the lay of the land from point A," Ghostman's voice transmitted to Blue Streak. "What's the view from point B, over?"

"Nothin' to report, Silver Lightning," Al's voice crackled back. "The best vantage point will be from the front, over."

Black N9NE looked at Ghostman. "We need two hittas out back to play clean up in case we get runners."

"Red wants no one to escape," Ghostman stated. "We got what —two rocket launchers?"

"Three," Black N9NE replied. "Anti tanks, I think."

"Okay, Blue Streak," Ghostman said, hopping back into the driver's seat. "We're done here for now. Back to HQ. Over and out."

(EIE HQ*Thursday 2:00 PM)

In a private room to the far end of the pool hall, eight of EIE's most elite killers met in a top secret gathering. Military grade weaponry was displayed on a long, fold up luncheon table where the men oiled and prepared them for what was codenamed OPERATION: BLACKOUT.

Present in the room were Ghostman, N9NE, Khadafi, Ground War, Eddie, and Monk.

A few of them had to whistle at the weapons laid before them. "This is impressive," Monk commented.

"Monk," Ghostman said as he pointed at the M82A1 SAMR. "Break her down for me."

"Yeah," Monk nodded and picked the mighty weapon up. "Semi-automatic, bipod, a inx scope. Caliber: 12.7x9mm fifty fuckin cal. BMG, ten round box mag ammo capacity. 1800 meter max effective kill range, 893 m-s muzzle velocity. 57 inches long. Single round per trigger depress. Special trainin' required for this weapon, sir."

"They teach you how to lower your heart rate, breathe, and more in Sniper School," Ghostman acknowledged. "Okay, Marine. Your mission is to get into position where you can pick off escapees in the rear of the target structure."

"Copy that shit."

"Ground War...N9NE," Ghostman called them.

They stepped forward.

"We pulled out the big 'Apocalypse Now' shit for you two crazy mufuckaz." Ghostman pointed at the two rocket launchers. "The M136 AT4 Light Anti Tank weapon. 84mm High Explosive Anti Tanks or HEAT rockets. Y'all familiar with it?"

"Yes, sir," answered Ground War. "Forty inches single use, 285 m-s about 300 meters effective range with one hell of a back blast. I'll handle it."

"The Ml41 Bunker Defeat Munition or BDM." Ghostman looked at Black N9NE. "Can you hold it down?"

"Is that a question?" N9NE smirked as he picked it up. "Single shot, disposable, extendable tube...Caliber: 83 millimeter high explosive dual purpose or HEDP with follow on frag grenade, 15 meters to 500 meter effective range. 32 inches as is, 54 when extended. Lethal back blast. I can take down the Secretary of State's plane with this shit."

"Eddie, Khadafi, Big Al and myself will be behind you as y'all send the rockets into the Villa," Ghostman said as he picked up one of four M-16s. "The M-16 with the 203 grenade launchers, semiauto or burst fire only, leaf sight 5.56x45 millimeter NATO rounds. 40 millimeter high explosive grenade. 30 round box mag, 12 to 15 rounds per sustained, 45 rounds per semi, or 90 rounds per burst. The grenade is single shot only, so we must reload after each shot. 550 meter effective range for the M16 component. 150 yard max for a point target. 975 m-s muzzle velocity. 39.63 inches. We can stand across the street, and blast grenades into Blackout's curtain covered windows. We've confirmed the glass is real glass. We'll blast the door off with one rocket."

This was not a mission for amateurs.

The meeting lasted late into the night.

CHAPTER SIX

(EIE HQ* Friday Morning*11:53)

Friday came around, and Joker was thinking of how he would establish his alibi for tomorrow's attack. The moment the thought came, he knew instantly how he'd do it. All bases had to be covered because all hell would break loose, but today was still today, and there was money to be made.

Joker had asked Frank "Knarf" Brown in his office to discuss his plans. They called him Knarf because he had a funny looking face, plus it was his name spelled backward. "We need a big take, so what y'all been scopin' out?"

"HSBC Bank on North Avenue in New Rochelle," Knarf revealed. "Never been hit, small police force, I-95s up there, Hutchinson Parkway, several quality escape routes...." he paused, then continued. "The plan is to go with a bomb and clean it out for payroll cash."

"A bomb," Joker repeated.

"Trust me," Knarf said. "We enter masked up, disguised down, and place the bomb in plain view saying: 'this is a bomb...we have a police radio...if anyone alerts the police, we'll hear the call go out and we'll remote detonate the bomb.' We take the money then

43

leave the area with a good three minute head start to the switch cars."

"As long as the device can't be traced back to EIE," Joker warned. "You know that FBI and ATF technology is cut rate. They can trace the paint on a thumbtack, let alone bomb components. A wire, a screw, a timer, to the fuckin tape. Don't forget the *Unabomber* case."

"The bomb is designed to trick 'em," Knarf said. "All parts are clandestinely acquired, and when purchased, raise zero suspicion."

"Old army trick?" He knew that Knarf was a Special Forces vet in the Army whose job was to dismantle IEDs (improvised explosive devices).

"You can say that."

"Do it."

"Already done." Knarf looked at his watch. "Our people sittin' on it right now waitin' for closin' time."

"Hit it and report back to HQ."

Knarf nodded and exited the office.

———

(Uzenna's Home*Queens, NY*Friday 4:00 PM)

Uzenna Jade had the ladies' attention as she spoke to all twelve of them in the living room of the Queens house. She spotted her sisters, twenty-year-old Iani Moses and eighteen-year-old Rosemary "Romie" Moses, coming around the corner to join them. Once they were seated, she continued addressing the women in front of her.

"Is there anyone here that wants to be free and clear of this life?" Uzenna asked the women. "Don't be afraid, raise your hands."

All of the women there were tired and weary of being whipped, degraded, filmed during sex acts, raped, threatened and made to feel fear all the time. They dreamed of normal lives where they made their own choices, had husbands, had babies, etcetera. Yet out of fear and trauma, they were still hesitant to answer.

Uzenna sighed.

"But where would we go?" Iani asked.

"What will we do to survive?" Ashley inquired.

"Are we gonna have to split up?" Diane interjected.

"You bitches got Stockholm Syndrome," Uzenna said. "Where you love your captors. Iani—what you mean, where would we go? When Giuseppe, Joey and whoever call you over to their house to tie you up, beat you and fuck you til you faint...and you like it—that's Stockholm Syndrome."

Iani stayed silent.

"We all stayin' together," Uzenna promised. "I won't let our sisterhood...and all the beautiful sex inside of it come apart. I'm in tight with some hardcore gangster mercenaries—more powerful than the pigs we work for. My man will put us up and make us rich. No fuckin. On some Cardi B shit: 'I AINT GOTTA DANCE/I MAKE MONEY MOVES/THIS IS RED BOTTOMS/THESE ARE BLOODY SHOES'. We'll live like goddesses."

"I'm wit you, You," Brittani declared.

"How sure are you about these dudes?" Val asked with doubt dripping from her voice. "We all been tricked by niggas before."

Several of the white girls in the group were so hood that they sometimes used the term nigga. They came from same slangs and background as Iani, Ronnie and Uzenna, and they had that urban/black girl swag as well. So anytime they used the term nigga amongst each other, the Moses sisters never even blinked.

"She right," Ashley chimed in. "We can go from bad to worse in no time. At least these guys are the devil we know."

"Trust me," Uzenna implored them. "These cats live by a code of honor...in the war against Al Qaeda and ISIS, they rescued women and children. So, I am a hundred percent sure of my man and the men he leads."

"He must want that sweet young ass bad as hell," Leah observed. "You give him some yet?"

"Squirted all over him too," Uzenna boasted. "And he has one of those big Wesley Pipes porn dicks with crazy huge balls and he cums buckets. I thought I couldn't take him at first, but he made me melt and opened me up in places I never felt."

By the look on their faces, it was evident that the women almost didn't believe her.

"You are so beautiful," Coral said. "Why can't I get a prince charming?"

"This dude is no sucka for pussy," Uzenna told them. "But what I build, I build for all of us. He's all of our prince charming. So, no jealousy. We ride, let's ride together."

"Well," Romie raised her hand. "You already know me and Iani will walk through fire with you."

"Okay," Uzenna nodded. "Whose in...whose not? Anybody who ain't in raise 'em up."

No one raised their hands.

"It's unanimous then," Uzenna smiled proudly. "I wish I wasn't sworn to secrecy... then you'd know why I ain't nervous at all. We have the firepower to overwhelm these dirtbags. That's how solid this thing is. We will pack on the low-low. We leave tomorrow."

"What if they check?" Louise asked nervously.

"They always do," Iani added.

"There's a Mafia Omerta ceremony tomorrow evenin'," Uzenna revealed. "I'm counting on them to call and order us to stay put. We have to expect a check. We play it cool...we'll have on some Jerry Springer or Nick Cannon. Food will be cookin' in the kitchen, no one lookin' like we goin' out...playin' it off like all is regular-regular."

The women were nodding understandingly.

Uzenna went on. "Late tonight, we'll pack only what we need and leave in Ubers. Abandon the Lexus, Coral. They'll track the GPS in it. We already have Brooklyn apartments all in the same building."

"Apartments already, Yu?" Louise asked.

Uzenna nodded yes. "I told you...this shit is real. We're locked and loaded, but look...once we're there for a short time, we'll move out and abandon our identities. New names, new everything. As far as cash goes, we'll be well taken care of. My man will take care of all our needs. If any of us wish to walk away, he won't stop us. He has a big money plan and hopes we'll be willin' to help him with it. If not, we'll give you a plane ticket and some cash, and you're free to go. Just hear him out first."

It was all decided right there and then that they were with the plan.

———

(Uzenna's House*Queens, NY* Friday 11:30 PM)

Later that evening, two Mafia enforcers arrived to check on the Queens Boulevard household that Uzenna shared with the other Villa dancers. The girls wore their pajamas to make it appear as though everything was all good.

It was anything but.

However, no one could predict the deadly events that would unfold that evening. The horrors began when the men decided they would "have a little fun" with Iani and Louise, who they caught fresh out the shower wrapped in large beach towels. The two men, Giovanni and Joey, entered through the back door of the large apartment.

"Well, hello, Mama Mia!" Giovanni grabbed Iani around the waist, squeezing her fat ass cheeks and jamming a finger into her pussy from behind.

"Stop!" Iani yelled at him.

"Aw, c'mon, honey," Joey said, slapping her. "You like it rough!"

Joey, who was fat Tony's son, shoved Louise into the room she shared with Brittani. There, Joey commenced stripping and raping her.

"Please stop!" Brittani cried.

"You want this Italian sausage?" he panted as he looked over at Brittani. She watched Joey thrust himself wildly, in and out of Louise's battered vagina.

Frozen with fear, she shook her head no.

"Then get the fuck out!"

Brittani ran into Uzenna's room across the hall while Joey continued to slap Louise mercilessly.

"Shut. The. Fuck. Up. You. Fuckin'. Whore!" he warned.

Iani was meeting the same cruel fate in the kitchen, where Giovanni had her naked and bent over on the table while he screwed her from behind. Giovanni was a large man, so he controlled her as he trashed her body around like a little rag doll. She didn't even try to fight him. Instead, she cried out for Uzenna, who sat listening in her room.

Uzenna thought of Joker, her John Creasy, and how he was her hope. Iani was her big sister. Her blood. It killed her to sit motionlessly. If she was gonna be a boss bitch, the Queen above all the rest, now was the time.

"Uzenna!" Iani whined. "Please! Uzenna, *help me*!"

"C'mon, girl," Brittani whispered desperately as Uzenna stood up. "What are you about to do? I don't wantchu getting hurt."

"Then let's fuckin do it together!" Uzenna hissed. "Enough is enough!"

"Oh my god," Brittani gasped when she noticed the switchblade. Uzenna was serious. "Whatchu gonna do?"

"You better grab a knife or somethin', bitch!" Uzenna whispered harshly. "Follow me!"

Uzenna crept into the kitchen, and her heart turned cold when she witnessed the scene before her. She ran up and stabbed Giovanni deep into the left side of his neck, striking his jugular vein. Dark crimson blood spilled profusely from his neck. She yanked the knife out with a sickening, slurping sound as Brittani repeatedly plunged the twelve-inch knife she had taken from the knife holder near the stove into the mobster's face, neck, and hands. Giovanni was so shocked that he could only yell once, before Iani turned her rage upon him. She hopped over his fallen body and covered his mouth with her bloodied hands.

"Give it to me," Iani angrily demanded as tears streamed down her face. "Gimme the goddamned blade!"

Brittani handed Iani the knife and watched her stab her rapist like a madwoman! First, she pierced the knife into his left eye, then into his throat and finally, a devastating death blow to the heart.

"He gone, bitch!" Uzenna whispered. "Let's get this other greaseball, raping sonofabitch!"

Iani held onto the knife while Britt grabbed the pot of boiling water from the stove and followed them into Louise's bedroom. Uzenna never hesitated.

As Joey held Louise's legs over his shoulders and thrust his bone wildly in and out of her pink pussy, Uzenna sneaked up from behind and stabbed him through the right cheek, aiming for his neck but missing. Luckily, Britt was there to sling the scorching hot water directly onto his bare back! He screamed like a bitch, letting go of Louise.

Iani pounced on him like a lioness onto her prey. She stabbed and sliced him up with unimaginable rage. It was a real bloodbath. This was the dark, gruesome killing of a man who deserved it. Demons from Hades were released from these women.

"Don't kill him!" Ashley yelped. "Let the cops have him!"

"*What*?" Uzenna had an incredulous look on her face. She used the switchblade to put a deep gash in Joey's throat as she drew the blade from ear to ear. "*Dead*!"

They all stood frozen before Uzenna snapped out of it and quickly wrapped Iani in a sheet to cover her nudity. Britt then covered Louise with a blanket that had blood on it.

"We gotta call the pigs," Romie urged them. "We have to."

"We way past that." Uzenna sat down, panting hard. "You bitches get cleaned up and dressed. Pack fast! If Fat Tony thinks Joey and Gio are M.I.A, they'll send hittaz. I'll take their phones and answer any calls. I'll say...I'll say 'they're drunk and passed out with the girls.' Meanwhile..."

"Police will think we ambushed them," Brittani said, shaking with fear. "We'll be arrested for murder."

Uzenna grabbed a fifth of the Grey Goose one of the men had brought with them. "Everybody take a drink. A big one."

They all did what they were told while Uzenna made a phone call.

"Somethin' bad happened," she said as calmly as she could when Joker picked up. "Bad, bad."

"Aight...who dead?" he asked.

She explained what had happened.

"Put me on speaker," he told her. "Y'all there?"

"We all here," Uzenna said back.

"Fuck them Italians," he stated coldly. "You can't panic. You did good for yourselves and for the world. We on our way now. Is anyone hurt?"

"We're all safe," Uzenna stated.

"Be sure everything y'all want is packed up," he ordered. "My peoples will come in, remove the bodies, make 'em disappear, scrub the place spotless..."

"They'll come lookin' for 'em," Uzenna warned him.

"Just grab what u need," he told her. "No electronics. They'll try to track y'all. Don't worry about a whole bunch of bullshit clothes... you'll get new shit."

Uzenna hung up and stared at her girls. "Let's move!"

Within an hour, several vans and cars from EIE's black fleet parked out front of the Queens residence. Joker hugged his woman tightly. One by one, he was introduced to all the girls. They loved him immediately. He was a hero in their eyes now.

In only minutes, the ladies were placed inside the black fleet cars. "Y'all are goin' to EIE Headquarters in Brooklyn, where my folks there have orders to make y'all comfortable."

"May I stay with you?" Uzenna asked him.

"You better not," he suggested. "Now you go head."

He handed her an M-9 Beretta. "You broke your cherry tonight. I knew you was a boss bitch."

She smiled and climbed inside of the LeSabre. He closed the door behind her and tapped twice on the hood. The lead car pulled off, and the others followed.

"Hey, boss," A-Son called out to him. "Did you see the fuckin bodies yet?"

"Nah, lemme look," Joker said, walking into the house.

"Ayo," A-Son exclaimed to all the other soldiers. "Them bitches *laced* them niggas, son!"

"Damn," Joker whispered as he inspected the bloody murder scene. "They sure did. Let's get to work, comrades."

CHAPTER SEVEN

(EIE *Brooklyn, NY* Saturday 7:00 AM)

The six spacious four-bedroom apartments were upstairs from the pool hall. They were newly renovated brownstones listed for rent by Jamaican Sun Restaurant, which was a property of EIE, Inc. Joker was full owner of the company and responsible for the building's mortgage.

"That's $4000 per month or $120,000 total to Bank of Amerikkka," Joker explained to Uzenna, Iani, Romie, Brittani and White China. "Y'all can share two of the units. They're all very large four bedrooms, two and a half baths. There's thirteen of you so, I'm taking one of them. Uzenna and her sisters will stay with me. Y'all will be good here."

They sat down inside of his and Uzenna's apartment as he sent a text to Ace who was setting up shop in another one of the apartments. Once Ace got the message, it only took him a few minutes to make his way to Joker. He let him in on the first knock, and the rest of the women came in as well.

"Glad y'all came," Joker said when they were each seated in the living room. "This is Meth Man Ace, a master drug chemist."

"What's up," he nodded towards them as he opened up the suitcase he was carrying on the coffee table. He removed a small spray bottle. "This is liquid crystal meth," he demonstrated.

He took the cap off and let each person in the room sniff the contents.

"Smells like faint alcohol," Coral said.

"I agree," Iani added.

"Aight." Ace laid tin foil on the glass table and a sheet of plain white copy paper on top of that. He sprayed the solution onto the paper until a light sheen appeared and soaked it into the paper. "It dries rather quickly. Once the op goes into full effect, I'll use airbrush technology and other techniques to do this to thousands of sheets per day."

Joker put on latex gloves and picked up the paper. "Acid-free watercolor paper absorbs best. Smell it."

"Wow!" Romie smiled. "It smells like paper!"

"Amazing," Brittani said, imagining the money that could come from this excursion.

"Will it ruffle from moisture?" Iani asked. "And won't they notice that?"

"Great question," Ace acknowledged. "But that's why I'm commercializing and industrializing the whole op. We'll have paper compressors to make pages look like new. And we'll manufacture paper that will prevent prison mailroom black lights from detecting the chemicals and also add chemicals that will cause K9s to avoid the paper altogether."

"In prison, a 'stamp' is generally fifty dollars," Joker informed them. "I know cuz I bought and smoked *tookie* as we called it, or *deuce*. Better known as K2—synthetic weed. The entire prison system smokes, and if we put *one* cat in each prison as our salesman, he or she can make a quarter million dollars a year for us."

"What about the meth?" Iani wanted to know.

"One hundred dollars a stamp," Joker told her. "And no, I did not ever try that shit, but the white boys and Latinos I fucked with in there opened my eyes to crystal meth and how El Chapo and all them other cartels are makin' *billions* off meth. I'm tellin' you, we gonna be rich niggas. Our K2 paper and meth paper will have fentanyl sprayed or soaked into it and that will hook our prey. That fuckin fentanyl is the key. That's all we hear about when they talk about cartels and heroin ODs."

"How do they use it?" Julia Miles asked. "We have smoked K2 flakes...but never paper K2."

Ace clipped off several specks of K2 paper. "That's all you need to smoke to get fucked up."

He rolled up a small joint mixed with tobacco and lit it up. Only five of the girls pulled off the joint before it burned out.

"Damn! That's fuckin good!" Julia exclaimed. "I'm high as shit."

"Y'all wanna hit this meth?" Ace asked.

They all shook their heads and frowned.

Ace laughed. "Just playin'.

"The smartest sellers will retail it in there for five grand per page," Joker estimated. "All we askin' is seven hondos a page, period. We don't care what them niggas inside do. Once we go national distro, we may come down to five hondos, but we'll see. Every other prisoner in there is tryna hustle to survive, so they'll spend whatever it takes to turn the profit—take the risk."

"And that's just the K2," Ace said, holding up a spray bottle. "This is liquid crystal meth which I simply mixed with a small amount of water and ethyl alcohol over warm heat to liquify it."

He took the cap off and let each person in the room sniff the mixture.

"My cousin Buck is locked up in Sing Sing," Ace revealed. "I send his wifey up there each month with a loonie full of heroin she gotta carry in her cooch. He flips it and sends home about ten to twelve grand every time."

"Wow," Iani said, interested.

"There are about two and a half million people in prison," Joker said. "That is an enormous market. With numbers like that, we can't lose."

"The federal and state government thinks the same way," Ace added. "They see niggaz as dollar signs on the new slave ship—prisons. The majority of niggaz are dopers, so we see dollar signs, too."

"So, we mail it to them?" Uzenna asked.

Ace reached into the suitcase. He held up a legal document. "First things first, we legitimize ourselves as a book, magazine, copying service for prisoners. Appearances are everything. Prison mailrooms have to trust us. We create a magazine, a catalog... simple publications like that. And inside we will have, let's say, page ten as the product page. The only one who'll know it is our guy or girl inside. If it's a K2 page, then they owe us seven-fifty. If it's a two-pager, they'll owe us fifteen hundred."

Iani piped up. "I get it. If we make a magazine about COVID-19 and being black and it has a meth page on page eleven, they'll owe us a grand."

"If that's what Red wants, that's correct." Ace nodded. "These are example prices for now."

"How do we establish contacts on the inside?" Julia asked.

"Carefully and methodically at first," Joker explained. "There are three thousand plus prisons in the US, so we have to bring the contacts to us. We will set up a legit prisoner's services company that provides social media and dating website management, pen pal services, copying, books, magazines, online research... everything they want. With pretty ass females as secretaries who will extract a lot of info outta them niggaz."

Romie smiled. "I'm really startin' to get it."

Joker pulled a wad of cash out of his pocket. "We'll be developin' all them ideas in the comin' days and weeks. For now...here, baby. Split this four racks wit ya girls for shit y'all need. Be frugal for now. Food, rent and utilities are free. Remember to stay off the internet."

"Trust us, daddy," Uzenna urged him. "We get it. The stakes are high."

Looking into Uzenna's eyes, which were as light and golden as her honey-colored skin, both weakened and strengthened him at the same time. He wasn't about to tell her that, though. Instead, he simply said, "Trust is earned, babe. You do that by bein' in charge of your girls. They're your responsibility. They trust in you most. I know I have to earn y'all's trust too. The first thing I must do is keep y'all safe. Help me is all I'm sayin'. Long as y'all stay low, you good. I got thirty guns out protecting this block and men that know how to use them."

Leah raised her little hand. "Like...y'all were...or are real soldiers, huh?"

Joker nodded. "That's right. Why you ask?"

She shrugged. "I mean...it scares me, but makes me feel real good inside at the same time. Thank you for what you doin' for us and for what you did for this country."

Joker looked at Ace and the two soldiers who had proud glints in their eyes.

Heavy on Joker's mind right now, however, was the big hit that would occur later on in the evening. Yesterday's bank robbery had yielded $200k, which was split between the six-man team and himself. Still, it was barely enough to run EIE and certainly not enough to finance his national prison plan. His mind repetitively returned to the full-scale war about to be declared on these Mafia splinter groups trying to run shit in New York.

Ever since John Gotti – The Teflon Don – died, these fuckin wannabe Godfathers were poppin' up, tryna take over, he thought to himself as he retrieved his jacket and car keys to the Buick Century.

Uzenna followed him downstairs, hoping to go with him.

"C'mon, bae," he said, much to her delight.

She beamed with glee. "Where we headed?"

"To establish an alibi."

Her belly flopped nervously at what would happen to her former captors later tonight, but she kept her thoughts and feelings to herself.

CHAPTER EIGHT

(The Villa Hit *Brooklyn, NY* Saturday 8:00 PM)

"China Brown downtown in position, sir, over," came Monk's clear radio transmission over Ghostman's earpiece.

Monk had taken up a perfect sniper position on the second-floor window of an abandoned tenement building overlooking a clear line of sight leading from the Villa's rear door. He set up the 50 caliber M82A1 SAMR, semiautomatic sniper rifle out the window of the second floor. He had already reconned the building for squatters earlier, but it was empty.

"Decepticon one ready, sir, over," Ground War said over the headset next.

"Decepticon two ready, sir, over," came Black N9NE. *"We're in position, experiencing a clear and peaceful night. All is quiet except the party inside. We are awaitin' your command, sir, over."*

Ground War and Black N9NE sat in a black van at the dead end of Livonia Avenue near the subway train tracks. War sat in the rear seats, holding the M136 AT4 84mm anti tank HEAT rocket launcher. He was itching to blow some shit up. This was the type of action he was built for. He had gotten his name and reputation from this very act.

N9NE sat next to him with his own 83mm HEAP M141 BDM rocket launcher with follow on fragmentation grenade. He was eager to go also.

In another black van were Eddie, Khadafi, Big Al and Ghostman with M16s that had M203 grenade launchers attached. Ghostman kept a close eye on the busy flow of cars coming into Livonia and Pennsylvania Avenues to park in front of and alongside the Villa parking lot. Thus far, Ghostman had counted eighteen Mafiosi vehicles full of mobsters parking and entering the club.

"It's alotta mufuckas," War whispered.

As the minutes ticked by, the excitement grew.

"Like waitin' for a rabbit to spring the trap," Ghostman said so everyone could hear his thoughts over the radio. *"C'mon, you fat greaseball cocksuckers...it's war tonight, boys."*

"Ayo, ayo! Down, down, five-O!" Black N9NE harshly whispered as he simultaneously ducked out of sight.

The others followed and rapidly fastened their silencers onto their Glock 25s. They weren't about to allow two beat cops to fuck up this party.

"Stay frosty, War..." N9NE whispered. "Stay frosty...."

The men readied their sidearms for the hit on the NYPD cruiser that, at first, drove slowly by the Villa and then came to a brief stop at the dead end. It eventually U-Turned and drove slowly back out to where they turned left onto Pennsylvania Avenue and disappeared up the street.

"Fuck!" War breathed hard.

Problem averted.

Once the coast was clear, Ghostman gave the orders.

"It's that time, boys, over." Ghostman put the van in gear and drove down Livonia, passing Decepticon One. *"Once you hear 'breach'....that's the go order, over."*

Ghostman turned the van around at the dead end and pulled in behind Decepticon One. "BREACH! BREACH!"

The murderous bombing campaign had begun.

(Joker & Uzenna *Teaneck, NJ* Saturday 8:15 PM*)

At the same time that the breach was going down, Joker and Uzenna were being cited by an NYPD officer for turning left on a red arrow near 59th Street & Columbus Circle in Manhattan. Once they cleared the area, they drove out to New Jersey to shop at an IKEA Furniture Store in Teaneck, where Joker ordered some items to help decorate the EIE apartments.

"I see whatcha doin', daddyo," Uzenna said, holding Joker's hand as they paid for their purchases. "The ticket is the alibi, and the IKEA store receipt...plus your *EZ PASS* is bein' recorded for the tolls on the Gelorge Washington Bridge."

"That's right," he acknowledged. "No better alibi than the cops themselves."

He knew that the day would come when he would need it.

(*The Villa*)

Both Ground War and N9NE were across the street from the Villa when they aimed their rocket launchers at the doors and windows. Then, on cue, they fired simultaneously once the order had been given.

The rockets ripped across the street and blasted through their targets, exploding with a resounding *Kaboom*, followed by a faintly smaller explosion, which was the fragmentation grenade from the M141 rocket launcher.

Ground War and N9NE then threw their rocket launchers into the van and bolted across the street.

They tossed a dozen grenades through the windows and doors of the now burning strip club as a dozen more explosions followed.

The survivors trapped on the inside screamed in agony as they became engulfed in flames. Ground War and Black N9NE moved out despite the blood-curling screams.

On Ghostman's orders, Fast Eddie, Khadafi and Big Al hopped out of their van to street sweep the men attempting to escape the inferno. Several members of the mafia came running out, shell shocked, as they tried to flee the flames, but the M16s did their job, rumbling and rocking the already violent Brooklyn neighborhood.

The familiar sound of the machine guns went on for minutes before the M203 grenades were launched—*boom*. It sounded like something from out of *Operation:* Desert Storm or Iraqi; Freedom.

Out back, using *Night vision* technology, Monk was picking off several men who were trying to escape through the back door. With the press of a trigger, the 50 caliber opened wounds the size of apples in their chests. Despite the damage he had inflicted, Monk had to radio for assistance. There were too many of them.

"I got runners out here, over!" he yelled and kept firing.

"Copy that!" Eddie ran around back, opening fire on all who tried to escape.

Back out front, a fat man came running. Fat Tony, perhaps? He was completely enveloped in a shroud of fire as he came out onto the sidewalk and slammed into a parked car, where he collapsed screaming *helter skelter*! Khadafi raised his gun to waste him, but Ghostman stopped him.

"Naw, son," Ghostman chuckled. "Let his fat ass cook."

The men all looked down at the screaming man, until his screaming stopped. Ghostman was sure he was dead.

"Aight," Ghostman said. *"Time to go mobile, over!"*

As fast as it had all begun, it seemed to have been over just as quickly. The vans pulled off into the night, leaving behind a shockingly macabre scene of war, death, and carnage, the likes Brooklyn hadn't seen before.

Police had been dispatched and given the description of black vans and men in black tactical gear. A city-wide alert was put out, but Ghostman had prepped for that. Only three blocks away, on Alabama & Sheffield Avenues, he had located a deserted garage days before that could store the vans and their EIE black fleet vehicles. The vans, of course, were stolen and untraceable to the crew.

The men undressed and stripped themselves of their disguises. They showered down with a nearby hose to rid themselves of gunpowder/rocket residue and dried off in record time. They dressed in fresh clothing and shoes and threw everything into the vans. Before leaving, Ground War placed fifteen-gallon gas drums in each van and attached small C-4 charges to each one with timers on them.

"We ready?" War asked everyone.

Monk, Khadafi, N9NE, Ghostman, Eddie and Big Al confirmed they were all set, they got inside the four EIE black fleet cars and left. Ground War waited to ensure that both explosive charges went off, engulfing the vans on fire, destroying all evidence that linked them to the crime.

CHAPTER NINE

(*EIE HQ *Brooklyn, NY* Saturday 10:30*)

Joker stood up behind the pool hall bar with his arms crossed as he watched the late news coverage. WPIX-Channel 11 News was dubbing it "The Mafia Massacre in Brooklyn."

Inside of their private club were Khadafi, Ghostman, N9NE, Eddie, Al, Monk and Uzenna. The doors were locked, the shades and curtains tightly closed.

"Shit went down without a hitch," Ghostman reported to Joker in a whisper. "We knew the news would sensationalize it, so we can't worry about that."

"The vans burned?" Joker wanted to know. "Clothes, shoes, gear —*everything*?"

"Everything, my nigga," Ghostman assured him. "ALL angles were covered. No GPS devices were on us or in the cars...*nothin'* can place us there."

The one thing Skeeter did right was prohibit OnStar and GPS technology in the black fleet, Joker thought calmly. *Police can track every move a mufucka makes wit GPS. Prisons are packed wit these dumbass niggas that roll with their cellphones on...never realizing that all they have to do is disable the battery.*

"This shit can't leave this room," Joker swore each man to secrecy.

"Under penalty of death," Ghostman replied with his right hand up. "No talkin'. You know the rules."

"Hey, baby," Joker called his girl over. "We're about to go on a trip tomorrow, so you and me gots to rest up. We're headed upstate."

She looked up at him with stars in her eyes for what he did for her. "Okay, daddyo. Please hurry."

"Share this with them, Ghost," Joker handed Ghostman a large stack of cash. "It's only a little taste, but bigger things are definitely comin'."

———

(*El Mira, NY*Sunday 12:00*)

They left the city around 8:00 AM and reached El Mira Correctional Facility at noon.

Joker had coached Uzenna, Brittani, Coral and Iani on the way. Now, it was time to turn them loose. They all carried double wrapped balloons with heroin and crystal meth stuffed into them. They were given instructions to visit a close war comrade of Joker's named Benjamin "Junga" Tines, who was serving a life sentence there.

The women registered at the Visiting Room Registration window in the administration building and were instructed to empty all metallic items into a plastic tray before walking through a metal detector. Prior to leaving the car, they had left everything except a roll of quarters for the visiting room vending machines. The narcotics were carefully concealed inside of their coochies over which they wore tight boy shorts to hold them securely in place.

As Joker had said to them, there wasn't nothing to it but to do it. They loved his calm grizzly bear-like swagger. Nothing seemed to put fear in him. He was a genius thinker and an even bolder doer.

"Stay frosty," he had coached them. "Be relaxed, hold firm eye contact. Don't even think about what you got in them pretty little pussies....them correction officers is fat and lazy, but if you act suspicious, they'll get suspicious. They just wanna eat pizza and potato chips and get through they overtime. So be cool. Y'all is some cold-blooded bitches who been through hell. This is like stealing candy from a baby. These pig and sheepherdin' hicks ain't got shit on my babies, so let's get this cash."

They were all dressed nicely. No one went overboard.

"Always keep in mind that the department of corrections is the largest police force on earth," he had warned the women. "Have some respect for that fact. No being high, no flash, always be cool."

They were eventually led into the visiting room, which was already half full with prisoners and their families. Joker noticed the two cameras positioned in opposite corners of the room. He strategically had the girls sit at certain angles to evade the cameras.

To the far left of them was a long row of vending machines where prisoners and their visitors stood, making various purchases with the rolls of quarters they had been permitted to bring in with them.

"Are we gonna hit them machines or what?" Iani said. "My stomach growlin'!"

"Fill the table with food and drinks," Joker said. "Y'all get to the bathroom and put all his shit in a chip bag. Bring it back out and sit it on the table like it's the most natural thing."

Once they did as he directed, Uzenna told the others to go to the bathroom and hide the drugs they carried behind the toilet. They did as she told them, and returned while she was standing at the microwave.

"The last stall," Iani whispered to her.

Uzenna made her way to the bathroom and retrieved the balloons the girls had stashed behind the last toilet. She opened a bag of Lay's Plain Potato Chips, emptied the contents into the toilet, and placed the narcotics into the bag. Then she walked back out of the bathroom to their table and took a seat.

"Where's daddyo?" Uzenna asked.

Iani pointed. "He left us. He said he'd be in the parking lot."

Uzenna was a little perplexed but decided not to dwell on it..

"That's him," Uzenna indicated with a nod in Junga's direction. "Follow my lead. Make it look good."

Seconds went by as Junga looked around the visiting room.

"Junga, hi!" Uzenna waved at him.

He walked over to the fine women. "Hey, girl!" He hugged each of them and kissed them on the cheek. "Joker has to be behind this," he whispered.

Brittani nodded and kissed him like a soap opera queen.

"That's enough over there, Tines!" the white female visiting room correction officer chided him. "You know the rules say one brief kiss and hug before and after...come on, now."

"My bad, Miss G," Junga smiled charmingly her way as she went on about her business. He looked at Brittani. "Damn, you taste good, look good...what's ya name, babe?"

"Joker told me you been down ten years," Brittani said. "Figure out a way to get us in the bathroom together, and I'll suck your cock, lick your balls, and swallow your cum."

"She's Brittani," Iani introduced him. "I'm Iani, and that's Uzenna. And yeah, Joker sent us. In fact, he was just here."

"Take the Lay's bag," Uzenna told him. "There's meth, heroin and K2. We made the balloons about the size of golf balls at first, but Red said you'd have to *boof* them, so we made 'em smaller."

"Yeah," Jung chuckled. "They gotta go one by one up the back pipe."

Uzenna laughed with him. "Get this money, nigga. You got meth, heroin, and K2. You stacked up real nice, too."

They settled down for a while and got to know each other. He sat close to Brittani, who held his hand and let him feel her up. He used her closeness for cover as he rolled up the Lay's chip bag and stuffed it into his pants.

"Okay, lemme break it down," Uzenna told him. "You'll be receivin' mail from several different sources. It'll be K2."

"Call it deuce, ma," he spoke low.

She nodded. "It'll be from us. The meth will come in a manila envelope. The deuce will come in a regular white envelope. We want a thousand dollars a page for the meth and seven hundred fifty for the deuce. All money is to be sent to $45redman...that's Joker's Cash App. That's dollar sign, 4-5, r-e-d-m-a-n."

"Got it," Junga nodded.

"He said y'all talked about all this shit for months," Brittani said, snaking her hand into his pants and grabbing hold of his thick chocolate dick.

"We did," Junga acknowledged. "So, the balloons...?"

"Yeah," Uzenna went on. "There's enough raw dope and meth in there to send him twenty grand and for you to mobilize all ya Crip bangaz, and get them ready for the ultimate takeover of the drug trade in here and beyond. It'll be your job to reach out to the gangs in New York's other seventy prisons...move ya bitches and henchmen near the prison to carry out ya orders. Joker wants this thing to spread and to spread fast."

"Um, damn," he grunted as Brittani jacked him off inside of his pants. "Ain't you all Joker's girls?"

"Don't worry," Brittani smiled as she massaged him extra good. His big dick felt like a lead pipe about to bust as she stroked it. "I only do what I'm allowed to. Can we sneak in the bathroom?"

"Lemme go first," his voice croaked.

Feeling a sudden trill, Junga got to the door marked "INMATES ONLY" and went inside. There, he waited several minutes and thought Brittani had lost her nerve or got caught. So, he pulled out the chip bag full of balloons and prepared himself for the *boofing*.

That's when Brittani came in. " We gotta make it quick!"

She went right up to him and yanked his pants down, exposing his flaccid member. She could tell right away that nerves had gotten to him. She started sucking him slowly, looking up into his handsome dark face. He got hard as a rock within seconds.

She lathered his entire seven-inch shaft with her warm saliva and ran her thick lips up and down and over his juicing slit. She moaned again and again as she took him into her warm throat. She caressed his balls and made sure she took both of them in her mouth while her hand pumped up and down on his thick lance.

"I wish I could fuck you," he whispered.

"Don't cum inside me," she breathed hotly as she leaned over and stuck her beautifully tattooed down south booty in front of him.

He snatched her dress up and pulled her boy shorts down around her ankles. He knew he had no time, but he just had to bend down, spread that ass wide open, and smell this pretty ass white female. He smashed his entire face between her milky butt cheeks like she was a whip cream pie and started sniffing and licking. Taking deep breaths to remember the scent of sweet ass and the unforgettable aroma of a hot wet pussy.

Seconds later, he was easing himself deep into her velvety feminine folds. He immediately started fucking her and holding on to her juicy breasts as he stroked her hard. But ten years was a long time without pussy. He could barely last three minutes before he pulled out. She quickly turned around and took him back into her mouth. Never missing a beat...he began to release thick wet ropes of warm semen into her throat. She swallowed him as fast as she could and stood up.

Just like that, she slipped back out of the bathroom and returned to the table with a huge smile on her face.

Inside the bathroom, Junga used the hair grease he had applied to the backs of his ears to lubricate his anus. Then one by one, he *boofed* each balloon up his ass until they were all safely stashed there. Once he had gotten them all in, he washed up well and returned to the visiting table.

"You good now?" Uzenna teased him.

"Hell yeah!" he grinned, looking at Brittani.

"How quick can you get a cellphone?" Uzenna asked him.

He waved her off. "With all the shit y'all just dropped on me, all I gotta do is make a trade for one in the yard tonight."

"Okay," Uzenna said. "Our B.I. is done here then."

"Will I see you again?" Junga asked her, but it was clearly directed at Brittani.

She laughed. "No...you fallin' in love wit it?"

Junga returned the laugh. "Can't say I don't love pussy."

"Well," Brittani told him sweetly. "We belong to Red. However, you get that paper up, he'll send you all kinds of pussy up here. Don't y'all get conjugal visits?"

He nodded. "You gotta be married."

"We'll buy you a wife," Uzenna promised him before returning to Joker, who had patiently waited outside.

CHAPTER TEN

(*Otisville, NY*A Month Later*Monday 3:00 PM*)

"What about this one?" Uzenna pointed out as she and Joker drove past a green and white ranch-style apartment. "It's on our list....It's a four thousand square feet flat."

Joker looked around the neighborhood as he drove slowly past the house. "Ace will worry about the area smellin' like chemicals cuz it'll draw fire or police investigators."

They were in upstate New York near Otisville, just due east of the Woodbury Commons clothing outlets. They were searching for the perfect place to buy or lease for their meth operations. Someplace that was secluded from other homes. They had a listing of properties that were on the market in remote areas with plenty of open acreages to spare, but nothing truly stood out until they finally spotted it.

"This is it, I think." Red drove up a dirt road approximately one and a half-mile north of the main road.

There were signs along the route that read: PRIVATE PROPERTY, and others read: "FOR SALE BY OWNER." The house that came into view was an old double-wide prefabricated structure that had seen better days.

"The house is not what I care about," Joker said as he eyed the property. "We can demolish that and have it replaced with a new pre-fab in no time at all. Nowadays, they put some pre-fabs together better than regular cribs. And quicker, too."

Uzenna approved of it as well. "That country road belongs to the owner of the property, according to the online realty report, so we can put up security fences to block nosey cops or neighbors who make the wrong turn. It's right where you want it since there's no one livin' within a mile of it from East to West."

They stopped the car and got out to walk around. Joker pointed to an old red and white barn. "I'm startin' to like it more and more. Look way back there."

"A barn," she said rhetorically.

"I'd tear that down, too," Red told her. "And likely put up an aluminum garage, fences and gates around it...and most of all, we have to create a business front—for the optics."

"I have an idea," Uzenna said.

He waited for her to continue.

"Auto body mechanic?" she offered.

He thought it over. "You are the cutest thing I've ever seen, you know that, babe?"

She blushed.

He smiled at her shyness. "You are one smart chick, too. I can really picture an Auto Body Paint Center or somethin' here. It'd definitely justify chemical odors emanating from the site."

He hugged her and pulled out his mobile phone. He called a number and waited until someone picked up. "Ayo, Ace. I'm textin' our location to you. Get here while there's still daylight left so I can see this through your eyes, will ya?"

"On my way this second, homie."

———

(*The Ranch house*Otisville, NY*)

They made the call to the owner and ended up buying the ranch for $195,000. Joker attained the mortgage by putting the EIE Inc./Jamaican Sun Restaurant and apartment building up as collateral for the loan. With another mortgage to pay off, Joker was far from worried.

The prison operations were rapidly bearing fruit as he had known they would. All day long notifications would light up his cellphones as the money came through his Cash App accounts. . Sometimes there would be $50 payments, then $100, $150, and another $100 or $500 which was usually the amount prisoners on the inside sent when trying to purchase "ID card-sized" amounts, that were sold for $250 per ID card.

Junga and his Crip gang homies were up in El Mira killing it. And through Junga's gang network, the operations had now expanded to at least ten other New York and New Jersey prisons where the Crips controlled the drug trade and funneled the proceeds to Joker Red's various Cash App setups.

After assessing the location, Methman Ace found that the ranch was perfect and wasted no time relocating. The first thing he did was transport his four full-grown Rottweiler's. For the time being, he kept them locked up inside the barn. Joker knew it would look good to have "white faces" up there, so he temporarily moved Julia, Ashley, and Eden to the ranch house.

"I have my own girls, boss," Ace told Joker.

"Good," Joker quipped. "You can keep your pipe outta them then. Thing is...your girls ain't white, mine are, so they stay for now."

"The plan is to rotate y'all," Joker informed his girls. "Learn all you can while you're around Ace. He needs all hands on deck anyway. Plus, I'ma need y'all to keep expandin' us in all or most of New York state's seventy or so prisons."

For now, he decided, only Uzenna, Coral Nee, Brittani, Iani and Romie would occupy the Brooklyn apartments.

"Expect shit to keep changing, though," Joker cautioned them.

"Today you're here, tomorrow you'll be there. A lot of cash is already comin' down the pipe, and it's what I expected. And wit more dollars comes bigger moves. I'll tell you right now, I'ma nigga who bets big on me. I get a hundred, I bet it all. I get a thousand, hundred grand, a million... I'm bettin' it all on what we doin', and we gonna get stankin' fuckin rich. Just ride..."

"You mind me askin' how much we made the last month?" Ace asked.

"Seventy-five thousand from the prisons alone," Joker said without hesitation. "With what we doing on the streets in a month's time...we talkin' a quarter million."

Leah and the other girls looked at each other with contained delight.

"Fuckin wit the Crips is payin' off," Joker mentioned. "See? Junga is the biggest of the biggest Homiez on the East coast. He Rollin' 60s Neighborhood Crips wit a lot of contacts, so I was lucky to be locked up wit him for my last eighteen months. But now it's time to contact the Blood Homiez."

"Why?" Ace inquired.

Joker explained. "I been havin' some block bitches take an ounce of raw heroin to Junga because it's a one-two punch hitta for real fast twelve to fifteen thou. But I wanna have Junga focus on the K2, meth, molly and acid hits we send him. Too much concentration gotta go into the diesel. So, throw that to the Blood niggaz. This way, all them niggaz can get paper."

The women were transfixed every time Joker spoke about money and his grand plans. They believed in him and were flabbergasted that $75k was made so fast from prisoners.

Ace was also sold on the plan. He was confident in what he could accomplish as a chemist, and he had a great business mind as well. With Joker's cash and contacts, Ace knew that united, they could move heaven and hell.

"Boss," Ace said. "I hate to bring this up, but I have all the creditors callin' and emailing me about car loans, credit card payments, my moms need money for her house..."

"Will five grand be okay right now?" Joker asked him.

Ace nodded. "Most def."

Joker sent Ace $5,000.00 to his Cash App right then and there. "Thanks, boss."

Once the money came through, Ace started to fill Joker and the girls in on the "regulatory" pressure from the federal and state authorities regarding crystal meth manufacturing. In turn, Joker wanted to know exactly how those federal regulations affected their operations.

"I need to *know*," Joker emphasized. "We just invested in a house and land, which are heavy liabilities unless they make money. And the girls are travelin' daily to prisons to open up new routes for us. A lot is ridin' on its success."

Ace nodded, understanding every word. "Lemme break it down."

He had them listening as they stood inside the Otisville ranch house. Its interior had improved drastically since the girls had been cleaning up the house.

"As you all know, there's this war on drugs," Ace started. "Which is largely because it's affectin' non-Blacks. Especially when it comes to hardcore, addictive drugs like meth. Crystal meth is high on the list of banned narcotics, but due to the ingredients used to make it, it's hard to stop its production."

"Why?" Iani asked.

"Okay..." he trailed off thoughtfully. "First of all, the ingredients are household products...shit that's easy to get. You just need to know how to put it together."

He explained that the chemicals used with producing meth could be grouped into three categories: solvents, metals and salts and strong acids or bases. "For solvents..." he started, "you got acetone, benzene, benzyl chloride, chloroform, ethanol, ethyl ether, freon, hexane, isopropanol, methanol, petroleum ether, and pyridine. For your metals and salts...there's aluminum, iodine, lead acetate, lithium aluminum, magnesium, mercuric chloride, palladium, potassium metal, red phosphorus, sodium acetate, sodium hydroxide, sodium metal...and for your strong acids or bases, there's the acetic acid, acetic anhydride, ammonia, benzyl chloride, hydroiodic acid, methylamine, perchloric acid, phosphine, sodium metal, sodium hydroxide, and thionyl chloride."

"I can't believe you know all that just off the top of your head," Joker said. "Amazin'."

"I ain't even done," Ace told him before continuing. "Iodine crystals are used legally for a lot of medical and commercial reasons, but they're used illegally for meth. There's what we call ephedrine/pseudoephedrine reduction method that *demands* iodine be used during the production process. To stay on top of the game, like the Mexican cartels do, this iodine is the holy grail of meth making."

"Iodine and red phosphorus," Joker said. "So these are central to everything to do with top quality shit."

Ace nodded. "Most def. Iodine & red phosphorus...let's talk about centrality.... The principal chemicals are ephedrine or pseudoephedrine, iodine, and red phosphorus. The required hydriodic acid in this variation of the hydriodic acid/red phosphorus method is produced by the reaction of iodine in water with red phosphorus. You wit me?"

They all nodded even though most were lost. Joker understood everything.

"Anyway," Meth drank from his bottle of orange juice. "That method yields high quality meth. This is what all the hype is about right here. As such, the federal government regulates the sale of iodine crystals, which are readily available for legitimate uses. It's illegal to buy or sell iodine crystals if used to make meth. So, producers get it from cartels, black market, or by purchasing and crystallizing iodine tincture, which is *not* regulated in most states."

"Damn," Joker said, crossing his arms while he listened intently.

"Regulation makes it harder to get. Why is iodine so fuckin' important?"

Ace thought about it. "It's used to make hydriodic acid. That's the preferred reagent in the ephedrine/pseudoephedrine reduction method of production. A reagent is a chemical used in reactions to convert a precursor into the finished product. Sorta like cocaine paste is the last step before the cocaine crystal step. The reagent doesn't become a part of the finished product. And the DEA's regulation of hydriodic acid rendered the chemical virtually unavailable in the U.S. To get around that, hydriodic acid is made by combining iodine crystals with water and some form of phosphorus, or red phosphorus, hypophosphorous acid or phosphorus acid."

"The reagent becomes a run off," Uzenna added. "Like a waste product or toxic sludge."

"Okay, Yu," Ace commended her. "That's good."

She shrugged. "*Are You Smarter Than A Fifth Grader*? I remember some of my science classes in school."

Joker thought it all through. "I had no idea of these challenges. I want you to scour the Dark Net and bulk buy all we need so we never run into production delays. That means the iodine and whatever else is being regulated. Shit, *guns* are bein' regulated. Cigarettes and alcohol too, but we can still cheat the system. Use your contacts and get us what we need. Can you handle that?"

"I have a cartel contact in Tempe, Arizona," Ace revealed. "Mexican military. I can fly down—"

Uzenna cut him right off. "And risk you bein' kidnapped? Daddy, he's way too valuable to send anywhere near a cartel member with the knowledge he has. You ever watch *Breaking Bad*? He's the crown jewel of the entire op."

"She's right," Ace acknowledged.

Joker agreed. "Yeah....think of another way to stockpile everything we need to make these millions."

"Gotchu," Ace nodded. "I'm already on it."

CHAPTER ELEVEN

(*The Paper Place*Nyack, NY*Wednesday 10:00 AM*)

Joker had Uzenna open up an office supply store located right off Interstate 87, New York State Thruway, across the street from the majestic Palisades Mall.

When the women were not visiting prisons, they were busy commuting to work at The Paper Place, or TPP, their new business. It was situated inside a strip mall area next to a pet shop, a dentist's office, a doctor's office, a postal service, a diner and furniture store. The lease was $3500 per month and the office space was 1500 square feet.

Within a few short weeks, the Rockland County store was up and running, with Uzenna assigned as its general manager. The other women now had new identities, new driver's licenses, and new lives. They still called each other by their real names, but in all other aspects, they had new identities.

Joker was almost obsessed with targeting the prison system, and thus far, it yielded staggering dividends.

"Hey," Joker entered the store with Uzenna on Wednesday with something heavy on his mind. "Get the girls for a meeting real quick."

The twelve women came into the office with Uzenna, each wondering what Joker had to tell them. They sat down and waited. Joker held up a box of magazines that had a shipping label from *Wallperiodicals.Com*. He removed each magazine and laid them neatly out on top of Uzenna's desk.

"Drugs ain't the only thing we can use to make money from prisons," he pointed out. "Within TPP, we are also a *Prisoner's Services Company*. Keep in mind that there are close to two and a half million prisoners in Amerikkka. That is a massive market! We'll be buyin' up ad space in these types of racy magazines. One such service will be our *Sexy Secretaries Services*. Y'all will be equipped with Bluetooth, so we never miss a prisoner call."

"The payroll, daddy," Uzenna reminded him.

"You are all salaried employees of TPP, LLC," he proudly revealed. "I want you each to set up your own bank accounts at Navy Federal Credit Union, give Uzenna your account info and your checks will be directly deposited into your accounts every Thursday. To start, TPP will deposit three thousand dollars to each of you."

The girls laughed excitedly and thanked Joker.

"Didn't I tell y'all bitches my daddy would take care of us?" Uzenna boasted.

"All y'all my babies," he told them. "And this is just the tip of the iceberg."

Romie kissed him on the cheek with tears in her eyes. The other women got emotional as well. Joker hugged and kissed each of them.

"Every dog will have its day," he said. "I love you girls. We saved each other. I'm blessed to be part of y'all's story."

He pointed at the adult magazines that were stacked on the desk, such as *Queen of Curves* and *Phat Puffs*.

"We can add or take away from the list," he informed the attentive women. "Most of these racy, urban culture mags are in every prison. They're what's called non-nude or prison-friendly mags. Not every prison allows porn anymore. That ban opened up the non-nude market."

The girls showed heightened interest.

Joker liked that. "There's a bunch of vendors who sell actual photographs of women in G-strings, thongs, etcetera wit barely nothin' showing, just like in these mags."

"That's two things," Brittani said. "Sexy secretaries and racy photos. What are we doin' here?"

"Lemme explain," he interjected. "There's a long list of prisoner services we'll provide. Sexy secretaries, typin', book publishin' assistance, editing assistance, three-way phone calls; email, social media, dating site set up and management, credit building...everything. We'll come up with a comprehensive list that meets the prisoner's demands."

He paused for feedback.

"Sexy secretaries is genius," Romie commended him. "I think they'll just call to flirt."

"That's the idea, babe," Joker winked his left eye at her and smiled. "Flirt back. Urge them to open an account with us starting at $15 to $100 and up."

"The underlying plan is to develop contacts inside three thousand plus prisons nationwide," Uzenna reminded everyone. "We been openin' up all these New York and Jersey prisons for the product so far, but there's no way to do the same thing we did here in all fifty States."

Joker nodded. "Exactly. So, our whole reason for bein' here, at TPP, is to have a legitimate front company to get us inside the nation's prison system. To contact and develop hustlers and gang members who will receive our narco paper products via U.S. Mail."

He looked around at them.

"Youse are all beautiful girls," he told them. "Y'all are 'ready-made' for the shit I'm about to have you do. That's why I'ma pay you like you weigh. Respect you and show you that real love."

The women laughed.

" Bein' a sexy secretary ain't shit," he said. "A lot dependin' on y'all pullin' this shit off."

"Demonstrate," Iani playfully dared him.

"Okay, peep it…" he cleared his throat first. "Okay, I'm sexy Iani without the pretty voice." He held his fingers up by his ears and mimicked the sound of a telephone ringing. "*Hello, this is iani at TPP, how may I help you, honey?*" he started, "The prisoner would say, '*Damn, you sound mad good. I saw your picture in the Phat Puffs magazine ad.*' Then you say, '*what's your name, sweetie?*' Don't waste no time.

"Pull up his account number, and if he doesn't have one yet, tell him how to set it up. He can send a facility check or have a loved one contact us wit a debit or credit card or Cash App—flirt ya ass off. Tell him quickly about our services in your sweetest voice. Make them think they have a shot to know you more intimately. You're single. Find out if they are hustlers. We *need* Crips, Bloods, MS-13, and whoever, as long as they tryna get that green. Feel out the strengths and boldness of each caller. No pussy ass niggaz or weak ass bitches."

The women were starting to get the picture.

"Invite them to call you again and ask for you by name," he coached them. "If you think they have solid prospects, give them a burner number. When they call on the burner, we get 'em narrowed down. That's where you lay it out: '*If you really tryna get paper, I have a way.*' If they wit it, then speak g-code. '*Find someone wit a cellphone or somethin'. We can make a hundred grand a year together if you dig what I mean. Figure out somethin'.*' And leave it at that."

Joker opened up the top drawer of the desk and removed a dozen used cellphones. "These are all burners. Hard to trace a phone they ain't got the number to. After establishin' the contact, destroy this shit in the microwave."

" You need encrypted cellphones, " Leah mentioned.

He looked over at her. "You know about encrypted communications?"

Leah smiled and shrugged. "A bit."

"She's a computer geek," Romie informed him.

He made a mental note of it. "I'll need a communications coordinator in the future. That's awesome. Anyway, girls, a real nigga will know when opportunity knocks. And y'all know how to use that superpower only females have to get a mufucka up under ya spell. Sell that shit cuz it's gonna make us millions. And so ya, don't waste no time on clown niggaz. Tell 'em right from the start you tryna be in contact wit the Big Homie Crips, Bloods, and First Crown Latin King and Ñeta niggaz in the prison, and if they do that, you'll reward them wit a fifty-dollar free services voucher."

"Good idea!" Uzenna exclaimed. "Cut right past the clowns and be like, where the boss niggaz at?"

He hugged her from behind and kissed her ear and neck. "Have I told you how great you smelled today?"

She turned around and said to him, "No."

"You smell mad good." They kissed as if twelve other sets of eyes weren't looking at them.

He was caught deeply into it, biting her bottom lip, sucking on her wet tongue, and moaning into her mouth. His hands gripped her full ass through her Gucci dress, and she felt his manhood growing hard against her.

"Daddy!" she breathed hard as he loosened his hold on her.

"Oops," he backed up. "Ain't like they think we virgins."

"That ain't the point," she punched him playfully in the chest. "They lonely."

"Oh," he said sheepishly. "Want me to holla at Ghost an' 'em? They ain't all got wives or—"

"David 'Joker Red' Hodges!" she scolded him.

"What, baby?" He played ignorant.

"They in love wit *you*," Uzenna told him.

"I...well," he looked at Uzenna for help. "What am I supposed to do wit that, mama? You my Queen."

"And I'm theirs, too," she said.

There was an awkward silence in the office.

"I don't wanna say the wrong thing," he said. "And come off self-ish...nor think wit my , either."

Uzenna smiled. "It ain't like that. We been doin' a lot of soul searchin' is all. We as loyal as they come. And even though you said we can walk if we wanna walk...the reality is, no one here will ever leave this tight circle of ours. We found a home in you, and these sisters of mine don't have no boyfriends... nothin'...just each other. And I'm okay with sharin'."

"You be our King, we'll all be your faithful wives," Romie blurted.

"Damn, Romie!" Iani said. "You see he nervous."

Joker smiled at that. "Well, I damn sure don't want y'all havin' strange niggaz sniffin' around all this sweetness... and I see my men buzzin' around the honey like bees."

"They sure have," Uzenna nodded. "But no one is disrespectin' the balance. We been talkin' for weeks about what to say, and it ain't just about lust and horniness. We see where this shit is goin', and we ain't tryna lose it to no other bitch later on down the line. We appreciate you and will ride with you...with our blood, our sweat, our tears, our souls and maybe our lives and freedom. But just us as your girls...as your faithful wives."

He looked around the room and couldn't believe his fortune. "I'll be damned...y'all serious, huh?"

No one said anything. It was already said.

"Hm," he muttered. He kissed Uzenna, then all thirteen women in the room. "I feel like I hit the Powerball. For right now though, let's get back to all this later and focus on this money. National ad campaign," he said, still unable to believe his luck. "Damn, I can taste all y'all right now...focus, Red! Focus!"

The girls all laughed.

"Mmm," Uzenna said as she tongue kissed Coral. "You better be ready."

"Stop that," he chided them.

"Okay, okay," Uzenna frowned.

"Y'all gone put a nigga on Lipator," he told them.

"We need professional photographs taken to use in display ads," Coral suggested. "Cute studio pix."

"Good thinking," Uzenna said. "Melodie, find a photography studio nearby so we can get that done ASAP."

Melodie jumped right to it.

"We can design a color brochure, info packet, application, to be sent to prisoners which will include our photos," Uzenna said as she wrote down notes.

"A list of all our services," Joker added.

"Everything we spoke about," Uzenna said.

Uzenna showed him what she had written down. "Price list, promo packages, deals, etcetera."

He nodded. "This is gonna be unprecedented. This Sexy Secretary thing—when they see thirteen beautiful girls, wow. I picture bein' locked up in El Mira and getting a copy of Prison Legal News, one of Mike Enemigo's books, SureShot, or Freebird Publishing that advertises the actual faces of the people I get to call. They gonna fall in love witchu."

"Aw, man," Uzenna said. "Sounds fucked up."

"Soft ass bitch," Iani told her. "We getting the money. Them niggaz and bitches on lockdown can get plugged up on our dating sites and apps. We got 'em, bitch."

"Fuck you, ho." Uzenna waved her off.

"Sex sells," Joker reminded them. "Since the underlying purpose is to find dealer prospects, we need to research other prisoner service vendors so we can give out the best prices. And we need to jump into the non-nude photos and racy magazine game ASAP. While y'all are takin' professional pics, create your own hundred-page magazine spread."

Uzenna held up a copy of Phat Puffs magazine from Suboworld.com. "You mean you want our asses up, cheeks spread, legs open, barely nothin' on? In a magazine?"

"Our own magazine?" Romie asked.

He nodded. *"Sexy Secretaries Magazine.* The *We Love Prisoners* issue."

The girls were excited. This gave them an opportunity to become models, and show their sexy side.

"Prisoners are sex-deprived, so a lot of masturbation goes on," he continued. "There are millions of free ass shots, camel toe shots, and more on the internet we can poach. We can do free pic promos."

"Leah and Louise," Uzenna glanced their way. "Y'all start scourin' Instagram and print out the hottest bitches on there. I'll search porn sites and print out still photos of bitches getting poked and suckin' pussy and dick. We'll use computer emojis to block assholes, coochies, nipples, penises, and whatnot. We'll push the rules to the brink."

"Butterfly sounds like a convict," Joker said as his cellphone vibrated in his back jeans pocket. He answered it. "What up wit it?"

"Joker Red," came the upset voice of Skeeter's mother, Minnie Dukes. "O'Mira's on the other house phone with me. I'll ask you one time, boy. Did you kill my son?"

"What?" He was caught by surprise. "Where'd you get that from?"

"The cops been investigatin'," O'Mira said.

Something told Red that the cops were probably there too, listening in and maybe even recording the phone call.

"Don't lie to me, Red!" Minnie snapped at him. "Them detectives said youse the only one with a motive to kill him because he snitched on you for the 2016 bank hit. And they know you led EIE back then. They think it's outta revenge that you killed him and reclaimed EIE."

"Cuzz," O'Mira breathed exasperatedly into the phone. "The NYPD gotta report that had Skeet tellin' investigators that your job was to burn the getaway car after the robbery and that you hid the quarter-million dollars. They think Skeet had the loot but sold you out to stick you wit the fall and try to getchu sent away for twenty years."

Joker smelled a trap. *"I did not kill skeeter and robbed no banks. I—"*

"They're here, Red!" O'Mira shrieked. "I can't do this knowin' that nigga was a rat! They recordin' us right now, Red!"

"Goddamnit, O!" Minnie shouted at her daughter.

Joker, seething with anger, disconnected the call.

CHAPTER TWELVE

(*The Meth Lab*Otisville, NY*A Month Later*)

Joker was pleased when he showed up at the ranch and the previous prefabricated home had been removed. In its place was a brand new two-story modern ranch-style prefabricated home. *These people don't fuck around*, he thought to himself as the final construction and landscaping was being completed.

Equally impressive was the old barn near the rear edge of the ranch's property that was completely demolished and all debris cleared. What stood there now was a gleaming new aluminum and steel garage structure that was blue in color and enormous.

Next door to the garage stood another, smaller, aluminum and steel structure that would become the Auto Body Paint and Repair Center front company.

Around those two buildings were high voltage electric fences with razor wire placed on top.

"We need an outer fence, without electricity, goin' around the electric one to protect people that wander too close," Joker mentioned. "I like the Auto Body Paint part of the sign there because paint smells like chemicals."

"To help conceal the real reason we're here," Ace added. "Plus, there's primer, remover and other chemical odors that come out of a auto paint shop."

"Let's keep upgrading security here," Joker ordered as they walked into the meth lab. "Aight, my nigga...show me the diamonds."

They put on protective masks first, and then Ace opened up a steel chest. "Ten pounds of high octane meth."

"Like that shit Jason Statham had in Crank?" Joker smiled.

Ace laughed at that. "Well, yeah."

"That's what I'm talkin' 'bout, my nigga!" Joker shouted, slapping hands with Ace in a high five manner. "Now we rockin', duke!"

"You could set the price at one hundred per gram, but since you insist on eighty per gram, that's twenty-two hundred and forty an ounce," Ace calculated on the handheld calculator he produced and showed Joker. "That's thirty-five thousand eight hundred and forty a pound."

Joker indicated the ten pounds. "So we got three hundred and fifty-eight thousand right here then. This is why we ain't in the coke game, son."

"That ain't it," Meth Man pointed at a large storage locker. He opened it. "We got about five gallons of top-notch K2 liquid nitro laced with fentanyl."

"Ooouuuweeee!" Joker nodded. "And what's all this other shit?"

"Ten thousand or so pages of plain paper pretreated with K2," Ace reported. "And another ten thousand pretreated with molly. All you gotta do is put 'em in the printer and print what you want on 'em."

Joker now had gang contacts in over seventy state and federal prisons in New York, New Jersey and Connecticut. And he was aware that Uzenna and the girls had already prepared and mailed out this week's round of narco paper to all of the contacts.

"Hot damn," Joker whispered, hugging Ace. "You're the man, son. What I'll do is move these bricks through street contacts. Keep stockpilin' and buildin' up the stash. We're goin' after a national takeover—so we need a lot more than this. Also, I'm taking all this finished narco paper outta here and storing it in the store mailroom. It's like a vault in there."

They loaded up a flatbed cart and took the boxes of narco paper to Joker's car. They tied them down to ensure that the papers were secured. Once they packed the last of it, the two of them stood next to the vehicle.

"Son, we have to address the obvious," Joker started. "Your position is unique in this organization, and I have to pay you accordingly. Five percent of all profits will make you a rich man if you stick it through with me."

"National takeover, huh?" Ace said to him.

"I'm on a mission, son," Joker nodded. "That get rich or die tryin' shit Fifty said. Only we ain't doin' it wit records, we doin' it wit bullets, bombs, rockets and an army of cold-hearted hittaz."

"Five percent sounds good as long as it stays between us," Ace said. "And when we get rich...let's renew the contract."

They shook hands on it.

———

(*EIE HQ*Friday 9:00 PM)

Every EIE member was in the poolhall. Joker Red's younger brother Big Al, Ghostman, N9NE, Fly, Lightfoot, Boo, Knarf, Blaze, Hard Knox, Bonecrusher, Broliks, Eddie, Big Chief, Monk, Mustafa, Ground War, A-Son, Divine, Ace, Uzenna, Brittani, Coral, Ashley, Leah, Eden, Louise, Valerie, Melodie, Diane, Julia, Iani and Romie. No one except Joker was aware of the fact that all of his women were strapped with M-9 Berettas in their pocketbooks to protect him if the need arose.

Joker and Big Al were on the sidelines whispering to each other. There was definitely some tension in the air.

"I need to know," Al whispered. "Did you murk dat nigga?"

"If he ratted on you, would you murk him?"

"Is that even a fuckin' question?" Al countered.

Joker rubbed his clean-shaven face before answering. "That rat sent the law to the exact spot designated by me and him to fire-bomb the getaway car. The detectives showed up like VD, right there. At my preliminary hearing, they said they received information about where I was disposing of the getaway vehicle. For four years, I knew he'd betrayed me. He wanted EIE for himself. The money, power and pussy."

"You coulda told me, mufucka," Al stated accusingly.

"Nah," Joker shook his head. "I wanted to be the one to bust them noodles out his head. You woulda took my vengeance."

"He coulda been settin' us all up over four years," Al pointed out. "That was some selfish shit you did, bro."

"Vengeance always is," Joker shrugged. "I ain't tryna argue wit you, nigga."

"Well, look around," Al told him. "You ordered everyone here, and ya boy Khadafi is the only one missin'. Guess you shoulda known that cuz Skeet was not only his right hand, but they were cousins too on Khadafi's mom's side. They were closer than Scarface and Manolo."

"Right." Joker unplugged the jukebox. "But Scarface killed Manolo."

The room got quiet after the music stopped. It seemed like everyone there held red cups with their favorite alcoholic beverage inside of them.

"Khadafi ain't here," Joker voiced his dismay. "That's unfortunate... and disrespectful."

The front door slammed. "I'm here, nigga. You thought I'd miss this circus?"

The 6'1" hulking man barged through the crowd, obviously high and drunk. He took a red cup from Eddie's hand and downed its contents.

Joker, annoyed by his behavior, boldly faced him, ready for anything. Each man in the room knew that Joker was not only a gritty street fighter and military trained close combat killer, but he also had a background in MMA. He never backed down to any man.

"Glad you joined the party, playboy," Joker said, staring him in the eyes. Getting no further lip from Khadafi, he addressed the group. "Most of you have heard the NYPD rumors that I allegedly killed my cousin Skeeter Dukes. From our sworn enemy, the fuckin N-Y-P-fuckin-D."

"So, you deny it?" Khadafi stated coldly as he stood close to Uzenna. "Joker mufuckin Red...the Big Bad Wolf. They used you as an assassin overseas, and you use those same talents on your own family now? You're the most ruthless killa outta anyone in this room. Own that shit, son!"

"We're all killaz, Daf," Joker was trying to keep cool because his girls were there. "We're more than brothers... we're blood comrades."

Khadafi took another drink. "There's killaz...and there's assassins. You assassinated our comrade...your cousin. That was your work, son. No one in here is that sick and brave to slit a mufucka's throat in a club bathroom. I seen the body, son! The cut was surgical...professional. That was you!"

Uzenna and the other women had their hands on their weapons. The tension in the room was so thick that it could have been cut with a butter knife.

"I resent the accusation," Joker said coolly, standing up to Khadafi. "I'm givin' you the benefit of the doubt right now cuz you drunk."

"Ayo," Boo cut in. "Word on the curb is that Skeet ratted Red out for that big 2016 hit."

"If that's true, we need to hear more of that," Ghostman declared. "And you need to listen, too, Daf."

"Son," Khadafi laughed. "Y'all gone believe that line? Joker is a *hunter*! He knew Skeet was runnin' EIE right, and he needed to eliminate Skeet to get it back!"

"Listen up you drunk bastard," Joker hissed, coming closer to his face. "Skeet never owned anything. He was my cousin, so I gave him power of attorney over EIE until I came home. It has always been my company."

"Daddy," Uzenna said, then whispered something into his ear.

"Oh," he said. "Britt, do it, baby."

Brittani unzipped one of two large duffel bags and emptied its contents onto the nearest pool table.

All eyes in the room watched as bricks of crystal meth tumbled out like big dice. Then she emptied the second bag, which was filled with cash.

"Ten pounds of grade A crystal meth," Joker told the team. "Valued at three hundred and sixty thousand. *This* is what I've been doin', homie. Preparin' the groundwork for a multimillion-dollar empire. And, the cash you see...everyone gather around and take a stack of five grand."

They each did as he instructed. Even Khadafi took his. Everyone inspected the bricks before returning them to the bag.

"I have mega-million dollar plans for EIE," Joker stared at Khadafi. "But ain't no room for disloyalty among the ranks. Anyone wanna challenge me...then let's go to the death. Right here, right now."

He paused and waited for Khadafi to make a move.

"That's that nigga's shit, son," Ghostman said, nodding towards Khadafi. "Red just smacked nearly half a mil on the table, nigga... you betta wake up."

Joker opened up his black blazer, making it easier to retrieve the .45 Glock he carried in his waistband as he observed the 9mm that Khadafi had in his own waistband. The girls were nervous, but they stood their ground.

"What up wit it, duke?" Joker dared Khadafi, dying to shoot his black ass right there. "What we gonna do? Blast it out like cowboys in this bitch or get this goddamned bread?"

The group slowly backed away from where Joker and Khadafi faced each other as several intense moments of silence passed by.

Khadafi nodded, picked up a bottle of Bacardi Limòn, and exited the pool hall, quietly fuming.

Big Al eased up alongside his brother and nodded towards the closing door. "We gonna have to kill that nigga, son. Word to mutha."

"Mm," Joker mumbled. "Stall him out. Let him cool off, let's see what happens."

CHAPTER THIRTEEN

(*EIE HQ*Three Weeks Later*Tuesday 2:00 PM*)

Big Al was chosen by Joker to oversee the street sales of meth. Once word had spread out across the entire city and the tri-state region, it moved faster than wildfires spread by the Santa Ana winds.

Grams were sold for $80, while the retail breakdown of each gram brought in $130. Red was automatically given a kicked back of $50 per gram, while EIE and Ace shared the rest. Al was opening up New York and the tri-state area markets for molly, acid and what became the best K2 on the streets as well.

"These white kids are *it*, son," Al reported to Joker weeks later. "They're comin' by the dozens from Westchester, upstate, Rutgers University, Seton Hall, NYU, UCONN, Pennsylvania, down Delaware—all over. They ain't the crusty, scraggly, white Brooklyn back alley junkies either. They more like *white-white*."

"Not white-white!" Joker laughed at him. "You mean like egg white?"

"Fuck you, nigga," Al elbowed his brother. "What's up wit the prison shit?"

"Expanding," Joker revealed. "You see by the cash payments y'all get how it is. We opened up new Cash App, PayPal, and Venmo accounts every week to hide the flow. Fifteen States now. Crips, Bloods, Latin Kings, Ñetas, MS-13 niggaz, and even Aryan Brotherhood. Real convicts with life, double and triple life. They getting it. Five figures each fuckin week."

Big Al whistled. "That shit coming quick and need washin'."

"Son," Joker said as they peered out the pool hall windows down at Willoughby & Fulton together. The block was buzzing with activity. "We're uppin' the production on meth, molly, acid, and K2. We need Hells Angels, The Breed, Mongols, and other big money criminal organizations to buy bulk weight from us."

"The dark net," Al urged. "Son, The U.S., numerous terrorist organizations, the fuckin Albanian niggaz, superpower nations, to the small backyard coca grower in Peru is movin' shit on the dark Web. If tanks and drones can be sold over that shit...c'mon, son. The monster has gone digital. You the one outta all of us wit the superior IQ. Get wit Meth on that and blow it up like the World Trade."

"We already explorin' that," Joker acknowledged. "Aight...you gotta bag for me?"

Big Al went to the office and retrieved a duffel bag. "Sixty-five bands."

Joker smiled. "Yeah, nigga. Prosperity."

———

(*The 74ᵗʰ Precinct*Brooklyn, NY*Tuesday 4:00 PM*)

"Lemme get this straight," Captain Miller stated impatiently. "You can *'feel'* that this frickin' David Hodges, aka Joker Red, and his crew of rogue ex-military vets are involved in *The Mafia Massacre?* What am I missin'?"

Detective Pope pointed at the big screen TV and replayed the video. "Sir...just look at them! Name one crew we know outta the city that can coordinate like this!"

"Walk me through it," Miller demanded.

"Watch," Pope said as the onscreen action attracted the eyes of over a dozen detectives who were part of the Major Crimes Taskforce Intelligence Unit.

They stared at an angle when observing the video of the hit team attacking the Villa from the street outside of the club entrance. It looked like a scene similar to the big North Hollywood shootout that lasted forty-five minutes.

"These guys are your decorated special forces vets!" Pope accused. "That's military training. Look at their *precision*... their *timing*...the *discipline* the *speed*...their *ferocity*. These guys aren't cops. We considered that. There is no doubt that they're elite soldiers. We spoke to their Cos (Commanding Officers), and most of the 'Everything Is Everything' crew are not just the best of the best, but baddest of the bad."

"Everything Is Everything," Miller repeated as he watched the video again.

"Or EIE as they are known in the street," Pope explained. "Started by our guy Joker Red. Superior IQ, a psychopath in my book. These guys formed a band of rogue mercenaries in Fort Green originally known as the HITTAZ, but they became EIE. We don't know why. However, The Proud Boys, Oath Keepers...fuhgeddaboudit. They have nothing on this group. These guys were used on suicide missions against Al Qaeda, ISIL, Hezbollah, Al Shebab and have some of the best snipers among them. Even the Commanding Officers we spoke to couldn't say how many kills EIE members have among them, but they did say that they are a gruesome group with a strong leader in Joker Red. They wanted to lock him and several other EIE members up for life but had no material basis."

"Wonder why that was," Miller said more than asked. "These guys are SEALs?"

"No SEALs that we can identify among them," Genovese chimed in.

"Army Rangers, Army Marine we have so far," Pope told him. "What worries us most is their knowledge of explosives, chemicals, and military grade weaponry. I mean, for Christ's sake, they used grenades and rockets over there. We need to arrest them."

"Knowledge ain't a crime," Miller scratched his head. "We're in the criminal apprehension business. What evidence do we have on them other than they look like they could be responsible for this?"

"Sir," Pope was clearly frustrated. "They fuckin' fired *anti-tank* rockets into a civilian nightclub, followed by grenades, machine guns, and *fifty caliber* sniper fire! Only one crew we know of could have done this! We studied an old bank robbery video, and these Mafia Massacre guys move in the same coordinated fashion as those in the robbery footage. I am positive, sir."

"I am not going into the DA's office with assumptions!" Miller barked at her. "A jury needs DNA, eyewitnesses, and fingerprints! Now go build the case!"

"Hey, Cap," Genovese said before they left. "EIE is growing more powerful every day, sir. They're building a methamphetamine empire according to what we're hearing on the streets."

"Since when do we give a damn about narcotics?" Miller shrugged.

The detectives were on their way out of his office when Miller called them back.

"On second thought," he said with a pensive look.

They stood at the doorway, waiting as he scratched his head.

"The feds are a part of this task force," he told them. "I've heard some whispers about this sex trafficking at the Villa....why don't I have official reports on this?"

"Honestly," Genovese hesitated. "We only just heard about it ourselves during this investigation. From Joker Red no less."

"Hm," Miller said, sitting behind his desk. "That's interesting... no women were discovered in the ashes. The FBI and ATF are wondering where those alleged sex trafficking victims are. Locate them, and I bet they may help us bring down Joker Red and his EIE organization."

"Great suggestion, Cap," Genovese agreed.

"I'm willing to bet my pension that you'll find a rabbit in that hole," he added as he walked them to the door.

"It's an excellent lead," Pope said to her partner as they left the captain's office.

If she only knew.

———

(*WOODBURY COMMONS*WOODBURY, NY*THE NEXT DAY*)

Big Al was called by Meth Man Ace to meet him at The Scottish Inn Hotel, a mile away from the I-87 North/New York Thruway exit at Woodbury Commons. Joker prohibited Meth from doing any deals with anyone due to his high value to the organization, but Joker had asked him to summon all of his underworld contacts in the crystal meth trade.

Big Al felt some leeriness as he pulled into the hotel parking lot with his 1981 Bonneville. It looked like it was on its last leg, but it was actually in mint condition, having been rebuilt with a BMW engine inside of it.

Meth Man met Al at the Coke machine in the hallway near Room 101. "What's shakin', homie?"

"Not this rinky dink hotel," Al said. "So, what's up?"

"I invited some heavy roller biker cats out here," Ace let him know. "They not only got big bread but big military grade weaponry and cartel friends that can get us the chemicals we need for high grade meth. I can only make the intro."

Al understood. "Let's do it."

They knocked on the door of Room 103 and were let in by a

huge young white man that looked like a starter for the New York Giants' defensive line.

Al had expected the typical long-bearded/longhaired biker type, but he was mistaken. The four men in the room looked more like construction workers than anything else.

"That's Spider, Wild Bill, Snake and Dog," Meth introduced them. "This is Al, Joker's brother."

The men all bumped fists and took seats before Meth Man excused himself and exited the space. As if on cue, Spider stood up and began to undress. "Let's get goin'."

The other three men stood up and followed suit.

"What are you fuckin doin'?" Al asked, frowning.

"What's it look like?" Spider shot back. "This your first orgy wit four white guys?"

Big Al didn't find that funny.

Spider burst out laughing. His men laughed with him.

Big Al got undressed and turned in a circle to show he had no wires. Once it was confirmed that they were wire-free, the men got dressed, showed that their cellphones were turned off, and began the meeting.

Cold beers were shared among them, and a laptop was opened. Wild Bill did most of the talking on the business end.

"We have heavy military weapons," Bill told them, displaying each via a dark web link he had accessed.

Al viewed them and nodded.

"Ace said you needed an unlimited flow of chemicals to make meth," Bill added as he tapped on some other keys. "Not only do we have weapons, but we have cartel contacts for iodine crystals, hydriodic acid, and whatever else you need for meth production."

"Aight," Big Al sighed as he leaned back in his seat. "Make this easy on me. We need five thousand pounds of iodine crystals and the same in hydriodic acid."

Bill nodded. "Fifty thousand in cash. Throw in a key of meth. How's that?"

Al agreed with a handshake. "Done."

"Now," Bill went on after sending an encrypted message order over the dark web to his people. "Weapons?"

"We're an army," Al shrugged. "So...the boss said to spend big."

"Big?" Wild Bill looked at his cohorts. "How big?"

"How does another fifty thousand sound?" Al suggested. "I want everything you showed me."

Wild Bill sat back and stared at Al. "We like people who deal straight."

Al nodded. "Look, man. Ace gave you the rubber stamp. So, don't gimme the mistrust stare now. We need long-term connects. Not a bunch of fuckin' wars wit you crazy ass bikers. We're all ex-military and we like to fly under the radar, okay?"

Wild Bill stood up. "We're from The Breed Arizona chapter, but we have a base in Albany. We'll deliver late tonight."

They retrieved their cellphones, and Al texted Bill the directions to the Otisville warehouse, which was in close proximity to the Otisville ranch house.

CHAPTER FOURTEEN

(*The Warehouse*Otisville, NY*Thursday 12:00 Midnight*)

Tonight, the bikers came in full gear, flying The Breed Motorcycle Club colors. Ten more men now rode in with the original four from the Scottish Inn.

But that was cool with Al because he had called up reinforcements of his own. The Breed were a notoriously murderous group, so Al was taking no chances.

At the warehouse security entrance was Bonecrusher, big and tall, all solid muscle. He had an M16A1 slung across his back with a sidearm holstered and a string of grenades hanging around his neck. For an added layer of protection, he wore full tactical gear and body armor. The electronic gates creaked slowly open and the utility truck driver was waved through, followed by two vans full of The Breed's henchmen.

Al and his men were all inside The Paper Place warehouse's main entrance, watching as the utility truck came to a stop inside, followed by the two vans. The Breed enforcers all jumped out, strapped to the teeth with AR-15s and other tactical long guns.

"So much for trust, huh, Al?" Wild Bill expressed with wry humor.

"Says the mufucka who invited me to a white boy orgy?" Al smirked.

Wild Bill liked Big Al.

"You ever wonder why they call a Mexican standoff a Mexican standoff?" Al asked Bill.

"No, why?" Bill asked.

"Because everybody in the room has a fuckin' gun," Al informed him. "A lot of respectamundo in that room...and not even the man with the biggest gun ever pulls the trigger. C'mon."

"Unload 'em," Wild Bill growled out the order.

"Help 'em," Big Al told his own men.

They unloaded sixteen wooden crates of U.S. Army weapons and boxes of ammunition. The Breed's enforcers opened up each crate to show off the contents inside. EIE men were immediately impressed at the array of firepower.

"Ten M16A2 assault rifles," Spider told the men. "Ten M4A1 carbines...ten M4A1 SOPMODs (or Special Ops Peculiar Modifications)... ten M16A2s with grenade launchers...ten M249 SAWs (or Squad Automatic Weapons)... the M24 SWS...we only had a crate remaining. Ten M82A1 SAMRs, aka Big Mama...ten MK12 MOD-O SPRs (Special Purpose Rifles). Five crates of M9 Berettas. Several Javelin anti tank missiles for armored riot or SWAT trucks. Several M136 AT4 Light antitank weapons...Several M141 bunker defeat munition...boxes of M83 smoke grenades, M67 fragmentation grenades, AN-M14 TH3 incendiary hand grenades, M84 stun grenades, and a crate of AGP DB14 door breaching charges."

While the EIE men inspected the new weapons, Al went into the warehouse manager's office and returned with two green canvas duffel bags. Wild Bill reached for both, but Al withheld one of them.

"Anh-anh, where's my iodine and hydriodic acid?" Al asked.

Bill nodded. "Show us the money and meth."

Al did as he was asked. He opened one bag, saying, "Keep that one...it pays for the hardware."

Bill saw the cash and the kilo of meth on top as agreed. He handed the bag off to his men in the truck and ordered them to leave. Al nodded at Eddie and allowed the truck to exit.

"Bring in the U-Haul," Bill said over his headset.

Minutes later, a second truck came in, and the EIE soldiers began unloading an enormous cargo load.

"Damn, that's a lot of shit," Al muttered.

It took twenty minutes to carry barrels, drums and bags of the various chemicals into a secure storage room. Al paid Bill, and once again, Bill sent his henchmen off with the second duffel bag while he stayed behind for a while.

"See?" Al shook Bill's hand. "We got ours and you got a hundred bandz, plus a key of top notch meth wit no cutthroat shit."

"Glad to know we can trust you," Bill shrugged. "Next time, we can do it smoother than this. We can drop off a load, and you pay us over the dark Web. Now we see with our own eyes...let's just say, we see a strong organization."

"Reputation is everything," Al said. "Put your rubber stamp on us, how we operate. We need your top folks inside the federal and state prisons to contact us at THEPAPERPLACE.com. We move meth, acid, molly and K2 paper products into prisons, jails, homeland security detention centers, immigration detention centers, private prisons...but only your top people."

"I'll be damned," Snake smiled as they looked at the business cards. "When our people contact you, they'll use our name."

They all shook hands once again and the biker gang sped off into the night on motorcycles.

Once the bikers were gone, Joker revealed himself to him men by dropping a rope down from the rafters and slid down to the ground below. He was wearing all black, full tactical gear, with an M16 machine gun and double Glocks strapped onto his sides. He greeted his crew with a dap before he inspected the weapons.

"Javelins," he smiled. "Incendiary grenades...C4 door charges. Damn."

A-Son tapped him on the shoulder. "Check out the serial numbers on this crate."

The green wooden crate that held ten M249 SAWs had a serial number attached to it on a silver metallic plate.

"FB-97-1483-MX," Joker read aloud. He checked the numbers on the other crates. "They came from different places...Water Vliet Arsenal, New York...to Fort Bragg." He knew the 'MX' meant they were bound for Mexico. There was nothing uncommon about that since the US sold weapons to the Mexican government. "Something tells me that The Breed somehow got 'em from Fort Bragg or the Mexican cartel who got them from the Mexican military."

Joker inspected the chemicals and had a satisfied look on his face.

"Nobody hear from that nigga Khadafi?" Joker asked.

Everyone shook their head.

Joker kept his concerns quiet. "A hundred grand plus a kilo was a good price...especially since we have a potential war brewin' with the Mafia. Let's get everything locked up tight and call it a night."

CHAPTER FIFTEEN

(*The Indian Sun Condominiums*Nyack, NY*Thursday 1:40 PM*)

Joker Red and Uzenna had purchased and moved into a four-bedroom condominium at Indian Sun Towers in Nyack, overlooking the beautiful Hudson River and the majestic Tappan Zee Bridge.

The ritzy development was fairly new, and when the opportunity presented itself to Uzenna and Joker, they didn't hesitate to buy the piece of prime real estate.

When he returned home from the arms deal, well after 1:00 AM, he expected his lady to be asleep, but she wasn't. Candles had been lit all over the condo, and he was caught up in the cornucopia of jasmine and myrrh. He heard passionate sounds of females moaning in the bedroom, and he knew for a fact that not only was Uzenna awake, but so were Coral, Brittani, Romie and Iani – all of whom lived in the grand 6500-square-foot residence with them.

Joker listened for a few seconds before entering, and smiled as he opened the door all the way. The living room and hallways were lit up by rows of candlelight and it took his eyes a few minutes to adjust.

He couldn't believe what he was seeing. First, he opened the door to Brittani and Coral's room, and what a sight to behold. Coral was behind Brittani, who was on her stomach with her ass up. Coral had her small right fist pumping furiously in and out of Brittani's dripping vagina while Coral tongue fucked her ass. He had only heard of women fist-fucking each other before but never had he witnessed it.

"Oh, fuck me!" Brittani whined, pushing her wet ass into the pretty China doll's face.

While Coral began slamming into Brittani, they heard him at the door and observed him holding his swollen penis through his pants.

"Keep goin'," he urged them on as he stripped naked in the doorway.

He heard other sounds of lesbian lust from the master bedroom and went to investigate.

He was not prepared to see Iani, Romie and Uzenna engaged in such sensual debauchery in the luxurious ultra-king-sized bed Uzenna and Joker shared. Iani was on top of her eighteen-year-old baby sister, making love to her with a black vibrating strap on dildo, while Uzenna laid off to the right with her pussy being eaten by Iani.

Three blood sisters.

The sight went straight to his dick and balls. Joker had never seen anything more taboo and forbidden before in his life, but all he could think of was how bad he wanted a taste of this sweet fruit before him.

He beelined to the shower because he wanted to wash the sweat and funk away. He was all smiles as the sisters.... then Coral...and Brittani, entered the large shower stall after him. They sat him down on the shower bench and massaged him all over. Uzenna took him as deep down into her mouth as she could, moaning loudly around his huge corona while Brittani spread her ass cheeks apart and tongued her pussy.

"Bedroom," he gasped into Iani's mouth as they tongue kissed.

They went back into the bedroom, to soaking wet from their brief show. Joker to in the sight of his girls and his penis throb with need., "Asses high...don't nonna y'all fuckin' move."

He popped a Viagra for good measure first. "Not that I really need it...but five in one night?"

The women giggled as he leaned down behind them and began kissing each ass before him, starting with Uzenna.

"When I think of women, I always think of fruit or flowers," he said as he placed his face in between her fat tattooed cheeks. He inhaled her slowly and deeply. "Fresh grapes..."

He tasted her asshole and pussy before moving on to Romie.

He held Romie wide open and smelled what she had to offer. "You make me think of lilies."

He then moved to Brittani and closed his eyes as he breathed in deeply. "French vanilla ice cream and apple pie."

They all laughed.

He kissed the left and right cheeks of Coral's fine tattooed ass cheeks before smelling her. "Mmmmmmmmm, pomegranate."

Iani was next. "Mangos all day, baby."

He was as horny as a young bull. He slipped his enlarged cock-head inside of Iani's wet cunt-mouth and pushed slowly into her warm sheath. He spat on his dick and proceeded to lube her up some more. She shrieked as half of his shaft popped into her vagina.

He squeezed her big buttocks and spread them apart as he started fucking her. They began smoothly and built up into something harder and more frenzied. He jack-hammered her until the drool fell from her mouth, and she climaxed all over his monster dick. Just as his semen was gathering in his balls, he stopped and slid out of her.

"C'mere," he panted as he grabbed Romie. "Can you take a real pipe, baby?"

Within a few minutes, Romie took almost all of him inside her tight little pussy. He let her go and slammed into Brittani, who got off on being choked and dog fucked. She could take a fist, so he knew she could take a foot-long black dick.

On his last stroke with her, he drew Coral closer to him as she bent over to give him a full view of her rear end. Without hesitation, he slid every inch of himself into her until she came so hard she nearly blacked out. Uzenna was playing with her pussy and squeezing her titties by the time he got to her.

"So, you and your sisters like a little incest," he said as he put her on her back and buried himself deep inside her.

She couldn't answer. All she could do was take what he was giving her. She stared up at him, and he kissed her sweet lips before tonguing her down like it was only them in the room.

Uzenna moaned with each stroke as she swiveled and gyrated those honey-colored hips around his porno dick.

"I love you, baby," he said as he began to fuck her harder.

"Oh, fuck!" she screamed so loudly it hurt his ears. He could feel her walls clenching him as she orgasmed.

The look on her face and those pretty ass lips fucked him up. He slowed down, but that didn't help a damned bit. It was too late. And the other girls knew it too. Iani sucked on Uzenna's extended nipples while Romie grabbed Joker's balls from behind and massaged them, milking him.

"OOOH, MAMMMAAA, I'M CUMMINNNNNNGGGGGG!" He exploded into a million stars as his man honey spurted deeply inside of her.

Uzenna rode it out with him, breathing so hard afterward that she almost hyperventilated.

"OMFG," Iani stated when Joker turned over on his back.

The women looked down at his manhood, and it was as hard as ever. The Viagra had certainly kicked in. Joker smiled as Iani hugged up against him on his left side while Uzenna took the right.

"That was so powerful," Uzenna whispered into his ear.

He agreed and kissed each of these beautiful women. Within minutes, he felt Romie sucking him slowly with her mouth and using her hands to caress his remaining shaft and balls below. Coral helped her by sucking on his scrotum. She then continued licking down past his perineum and into his anal cavity. Iani sat her wet pussy on his face, ass first.

Uzenna and Brittani made love to each other next to them.

"I wanna smell like your cunt and daddy's cum," Brittani said to Uzenna as she put her face between Uzenna's legs.

Twenty minutes into this round, Joker was on top of Romie long-dicking her tight young pussy with all he had.

"Cum inside of her, daddy," Uzenna urged him on. "Cum deep inside of my baby sister."

He did exactly as she'd urged him to, and once they were done, he cradled Romie in his arms and kissed her. Brittani left and returned with bottles of cold water and beer in a champagne bucket full of ice.

This time, it was Uzenna who got between Romie's legs and licked her swollen pussy as she tried to eat all of his semen out of her. He watched, and his penis got extremely hard all over again.

"That shit blows my mind," he stated. "This forbidden, taboo shit...I never thought..."

"Get used to it," Uzenna warned him. "Me and my sisters can't get enough of each other. "

"Is she on birth control?" he wanted to know.

Romie answered for herself. "No."

"What am I not getting?" he asked. "No condoms in sight. You told me to cum in her."

Uzenna sat up and put on a T-shirt. The other girls followed suit.

"Alright," Uzenna sighed. "I'm pregnant with your child."

He was stunned.

Now it was his turn to sit up and pull the covers over himself to hide his still hard penis.

"That's what's up!" he laughed.

She kissed him but kept a semi-serious look on her face. "We're layin' it all out right here. We all been talking...all thirteen of us. Whatchu see wit me, Iani and Romie....we close sexually wit' all the girls. Coral was kinda voted in about four years ago, but we a tight clique. We a clan. We have a pact, a bond to stay together always."

"Okay," he said, nodding. "And I support that."

"Well..." she said. "We all wanna belong exclusively to you. And not just a sex thing, or business thing...but blood."

He thought about it. "Thirteen women is a lot but all y'all my babies."

"You be our leader and king and we'll be all yours," Uzenna said. "We want some semblance of a normal life..."

Iani clarified it more. "But we can't have regular normal like a boyfriend or husband...and all of this. We have you and we love you."

"Well, now that we are yours, daddy, we need somethin' in return... since we givin' you all of us," Coral added. "You get loyalty, submission, ride or die bad young bitches."

"What do you need for you to trust me?" he asked.

"We all need your babies," Uzenna dropped the bombshell. "That's the blood. We're one family now. Let's keep it that way. Our kids will all have one daddy and be brothers and sisters."

Joker was quiet for a while, thoughtful. "And y'all are unanimous on this?"

"All thirteen of us," Uzenna said, lying back down next to him.

"I'd be honored to be y'all kid's father," he told them. "Y'all see what a nigga workin' wit? I'm a porno star master love maker wit mad cum all day every day, so that ain't gonna be no problem!"

The two kissed to seal the deal.

"As a matter of fact," Joker got up and made her stand up. He got down on one knee. "Uzenna Jade, will you be my wife?"

She nodded. "Yes!"

"I'll buy your ring today," he promised as the other women clapped their hands delightfully.

"As for y'all..." he thought aloud. "The laws won't allow us to be married, but we gonna have our own ceremony before God because *he's* the real King anyway. Uzenna the Queen among y'all, so in the eyes of the law, she'll be the wife. In our household, you'll be the sister wives where you'll be equal."

Romie rolled over on her back with her legs up as a blissful smile formed on her face.

"Whatchu doin', lil hot ass?" Uzenna asked her.

"Tryna keep daddy's seed in there so I get pregnant next," Romie grinned mischievously.

Joker pulled the sheet off of his frame and displayed his hardened shaft. "No worries, baby girl, cuz what I got—my dick touchin' the egg."

They made love well after the sun came up.

CHAPTER SIXTEEN

(*The Indian Sun Condos*Later That Day*)

Joker sat transfixed by what was being said while all thirteen women were curled up either on the 12' x 14' ultra-king-sized bed or lounged around on the comfortable bedside sofas talking candidly about their lives.

"The world will never understand us," Romie said tearfully. " They'll burn us at the stake like witches because of the prostitution and incest."

"But we're truly in love with each other," Iani defended how they felt. "What the fuck do they know about what we been through? Or where we came from?"

"You're the oldest girl, yeah?" Joker asked.

"I'm twenty," Iani nodded. "Our dad started with me. At three, I was already giving him blow jobs. At five, he was fuckin' me and givin' me gifts and candy. I thought it was normal. I didn't know it, but he was doin' the same things to my sisters."

"He was shot and killed when we were sent to live with his brother Aaron," Uzenna added. "You'd think it was gonna continue with Aaron, but it was his wife who wanted us. She kicked him out and started in on me."

"She wouldn't feed us if we didn't please her," Iani said. "Then she pimped me out to her cousin, her own father, and her uncles. Next thing you know, we were bein' passed around through her entire family. Seven years old, eight, nine, ten, eleven...we never even saw the inside of a high school."

"There was a big house fire," Romie explained, looking furtively at Uzenna. She hesitated, thinking maybe she was saying too much.

The women got quiet then.

Uzenna finished the story. "We ran away when we were eleven, twelve, and thirteen. "

Joker stopped her. "The fire was at Aaron's wife's house? What happened in the fire? Anybody die?"

Uzenna nodded. "Everyone in the house died."

Joker had a somber look on his face. He decided not to push it. "Aight...so y'all ran away."

Romie continued. "While we hopped around Mississippi, we eventually learned about Craigslist and Backpage. This Italian guy paid us a lot of money to strip in a private club in Biloxi...for older men who wanted under aged girls."

"We ended up in New Orleans on a large casino boat," Uzenna shrugged. "Basically kidnapped. That's where we met our white girls and a dozen or so other women."

"What happened to them?" Joker wanted to know.

Uzenna looked at him. "Dead...them ruthless bastards killed them girls like dogs."

Joker knew that the conversation had the women reliving one traumatic experience after the other. Not wishing to upset them any further, he told them to get in the bed, underneath the covers.

"We just chillin here all day," he said as he welcomed Diane, Mel and Leah in beside the rest of them. " We got money, weed, food, drinks...and each other. We family now. And I vow to *murder* anyone who tries to ever harm any of you again. I love y'all."

Oh what a tangled web we weave. Uzenna thought.

CHAPTER SEVENTEEN

(*The Paper Place*Nyack, NY*12:30 PM)

"We're in most of the urban street culture magazines in the country now," Uzenna smiled satisfactorily at her twelve sister wives. They all crowded around her desk and examined the glossy colorful photographs being used in TPPs national ad campaign. "I'm really proud of how gorgeous we all look...especially in the *Sexy Secretaries* ads."

"When do the first magazines hit the stores?" Leah asked.

"Many of 'em will be out late November for the December issue," Uzenna said. "Other magazine release dates differ. For instance, *Queen of Curves* comes out November 23...*Straight Stunting, Don Diva, Prison Legal News, Bootylicious, Felon, F.E.D.S.* and *Phat Puffs* come out November 28th. All around the last week of the month they're distributed nationally."

As sales from the prisons surpassed the five-figure per week mark, and hundreds of thousands came in from street and dark web sales, Joker's company was well positioned to spend over $100k on advertising in forty magazines nationwide. Careful not to use cash, TPP, instead, used the company credit and loans to purchase its ads for purposes of legitimacy.

"At every turn use credit lines for everything," Joker instructed his women. "Legally, we don't have the hundred k to spend. We actually have over half a milly tucked, but the IRS don't know that. Let the world think we have a 100k in credit debt because that's just superior intellect at work."

"Sheesh!" Louise smiled big. "That's a lotta debt."

"Not when we pay the minimum owed," Joker quipped. "In some cases, we pay $7500—the minimum each month. In other cases, we obtain a new loan to pay more on the old debt...to make us *appear* like we're great credit line candidates. We'll pay $30,000 on the original debt amount instead of the $7500 minimum. See? Then a company like Capital One sees us pay 30k on the 60k we owe, and they throw us an even bigger increase next time."

"Using their money to pay them," Uzenna added. "Using Visa cash to pay off MasterCard and MasterCard to pay off Amerikkkan Express, etcetera. All the while, our capital grows."

"It's a math game," Joker continued. "While we *could* pay all debt off today...why pay it when it could get us in trouble?"

Joker sauntered behind the women that gathered before the wide-screen computer to get a peek at the images they were staring at.

He had also taken notice of the colorful array of brochures and beautiful studio photographs laid out all across the desktop and was pleased with what he was seeing.

"Aight...good fuckin' job," he approved. "So...these are the magazine ads, the studio photographs, and brochures for *Sexy Secretaries?*"

Uzenna nodded. "You like?"

He shrugged. "I was thinking more like y'all showin' off some camel toe, some booty cheeks in the brochures. These are pretty, girl next door..."

Leah punched him in the arm. "C'mon, daddy...for the intro? It'll look fake...like we catfishin'. This looks real."

He ended up giving the go ahead. "Well, the boat's left the port anyway, so I think it'll be a success. I just hope y'all don't get lazy when the mail starts coming in like crazy and the phones start ringin' like a three-alarm fire."

"We ain't," Leah promised. "I'm tryna get this Birkin bag, so I'm comin' to work. Just don't get lazy wit that paycheck!"

They all shared a laugh.

"Ha, ha, Blondie got jokes," Joker smiled and grabbed her from behind.

As he did that, Iani's lustful eyes found his. Romie took notice of how sexy he looked, wishing he would take her home and bury his porno king dick inside of her, but it wasn't her turn.

After their meeting, Joker left with Leah, Diane, Melodie and Valerie. That's how he would always do it. He could ejaculate four times per day so he would be sure to deposit his seed in at least four of his women. He was living a complete fantasy.

CHAPTER EIGHTEEN

(*Brownsville*Brooklyn, NY*Thursday, 9:07*)

Big Al was headed into Brownsville, making several heroin, molly, acid, K2 and crystal meth deliveries. He was using an uber car for transportation, seated in the back seat while talking on a hands-free headset to a schoolteacher at P.S 41.

The white male teacher wanted two grams of the meth and a bundle (ten bags) of the heroin. The Uber turned off of Mother Gaston Avenue and onto Lott Avenue. Big Al, distracted by the phone call, did not notice the surreptitious tail. It was dark outside, made even darker by the thick snow cloud which covered the sky.

The Uber, a red Equinox, took a right turn onto Rockaway Avenue and then another quick right onto Newport Avenue. The Equinox slowed to allow two young boys to cross the street before it turned left onto Thatford Avenue.

Public School 41 occupied the entire length of Thatford, which came to a stop at Riverdale Avenue. In the rear of the school was "41 Park," where the uber ride came to a stop.

"Hold up a sec, homie," Big Al ordered the Puerto Rican driver.

Al never did see the shadowy hitta creeping up from the right side of the SUV, brandishing a semiautomatic tech nine. The hitta unloaded on Al with red kisses of fire, spitting from the silenced barrel of the gun before he had a chance to react.

A rain of bullets pierced the windows, and the glass shattered into a million pieces. Four rounds managed to hit each man during the onslaught while their bodies shook like 50,000 volts of electricity had been coursing through them.

The dark figure emerged, dressed in black tactical gear, coming in to see if there was any sign of life. Big Al, miraculously, had survived the ambush. The hitta raised his weapon, trained it at Al's head, and stopped in his tracks.

A pair of headlights had turned onto Thatford Avenue. The shadowy assassin swiftly ran through 41 Park, escaping in the darkness like a stealthy black cat. Big Al, mortally wounded, managed to call Joker's number.

"Red..." Al forced out in a strained voice. "I'm...I'm.....hit...."

"What!" Red had to hush the girls. "You said you was *hit*, nigga? You mean *shot*?"

"Yeah..." Al was losing consciousness fast. "Sorry, bro..."

There was a pause.

"Where you at?"

"That nigga....Khadafi...." was Al's last words.

"Al! Ayo, Al!"

But Al was dead...

Joker stared at the phone, stunned.

CHAPTER NINETEEN

(*EIE HQ*Brooklyn, NY*Friday 2:30 PM*)

"Big Al was ambushed and executed by Khadafi," Ghostman stated angrily at the EIE emergency meeting. "Supposedly outta revenge for Red hitting Skeet."

"What?" A-Son's mouth dropped. "They all fuckin related. God, are you kiddin' me right now?"

"Damn!" Blaze shook his head.

"Yeah, he had to really sneak up on Al, cuz son a gunfighter for real," Ground War said sadly.

"We out here getting rich, stackin' all this paper, and son does this shit?" N9NE added in disbelief.

"Khadafi did exactly what he accused Red of!" A-Son was getting angrier. "Over a cat that got a *rat* tag on him?"

Ghostman looked over at Joker, who sat in deadly silence with double Glocks visible in his waistband.

"Anything you want, boss." Ghostman was ready to *go*. "It's whatever."

"Angel," Joker growled.

The soldiers stared blankly at him.

"Angel?" Ghost repeated. Then, suddenly it dawned on him. "His baby mama."

"Snatch that bitch up," Joker ordered with tears of fury in his eyes. "Get their fuckin' son, too."

"He also has mistresses..." Joker continued. "Don't be sloppy. Leave no bodies, no evidence, burn Brooklyn down tonight."

"Y'all heard the boss," Ghost ordered, standing up. "We need stolen cars, electric saws, the whole nine. Let's roll!"

Joker stopped them. "Ten grand to every man here for the work. Fifty grand to the man or men who kills Khadafi. Seventy-five grand if I can get him alive."

"Son, I gotta say this," Ghostman started. "You niggaz was related by a stepfather, so he ain't ya blood. But some of the mufuckas we gonna run into will be your blood."

Joker placed one hand behind Ghostman's neck and pulled his forehead up against his for several seconds before speaking.

"My blood is my comrades in this room," Joker stated clearly. "Al was not just my blood brother. He was our blood comrade. My loyalty is with EIE. Just cuz family is blood doesn't mean they family. Do what the fuck y'all need out there."

It was revenge night in Brooklyn.

Joker was about to exit EIE headquarters when he returned to Ghostman and Black N9NE. "Y'all niggaz need to listen. There needs to be a clear hierarchy of power when I'm not around so there's no confusion."

"You're the boss," N9NE said.

"I'm not talkin' bout me," Joker stated. "Ghost is underboss. N9NE is a Captain."

N9NE was honored and said as much. "That means a lot to me, boss. Copy dat shit."

Everyone slapped Ghost and N9NE on their backs and shook their hands.

"A-Son, War, Monk, Eddie, y'all come wit me," Joker said.

Ghostman ordered the rest to gear up.

Joker went outside with A-Son, Eddie, War and Monk close behind him. They cautiously scanned the block to ensure Khadafi was nowhere in sight. For added measures, Joker checked rooftop positions since most of the EIE were trained marksmen who could handle a rifle well.

"This shit stops nothing," Joker spoke out defiantly to his five-man group once it was clear. "We blowin' up like I thought we would. Spread the word, son. We a million-dollar empire now."

Fast Eddie's eyebrows rose. "Don't fuck around, Red. You got a million dollars stacked? *Seven zeros.*"

Red nodded. "Ain't nobody fuckin around, nigga. I told y'all this goddamn narco paper move and international dark web sales would catapult us into a major crime syndicate. And we just getting started."

"You got it poppin'," A-Son commended him.

"We got it poppin', homie," Joker corrected him.

Aside from the growing list of prison contacts, The Paper Place's services, and street sales, Meth Man Ace was responsible for establishing the gang members that he knew:

MOTORCYCLE GANGS:

Bandidos, Brothers Speed, Chosen Few, Devil's Disciples, East Bay Dragons, Free Souls, Gypsy Jokers, Hells Angels, Highwaymen, Iron Horsemen, Mongols, Outlaws, Pagans, Vagos and Warlocks.

"EIE ain't fuckin around. I'm talkin' *millions.* Word is out to all street gangs and crime bosses that EIE got cartel level weight, and it's about time we hired mercenaries to help handle the load. There's strength in numbers, and we gonna need 'em."

"All street gangs?" Eddie repeated.

Joker pulled up a text he was sent by Meth Man Ace, showing the lists of gangs that he knew. Joker held up the phone so the boys had a better view.

ASIANS:

Asian Boys

Jackson Street Boys

Kkangpae
Menace of Destruction
Triads
Yakuza
Wah Ching
Tiny Rascal Gang

"That's just the Asian gangs," Joker paused as he swiped down the touchscreen to show them even more. "We're targeting all of 'em except for the Italians because we can't trust them right now."

A-Son read what was on the lists. "Albanians, Irish Mafia... there's a lotta Latino gangs here. Middle Eastern Israeli Mafia—I ain't even know the Israelis had a Mafia... there's mad prison gangs. The Russian and Polish Mafias... Aryans and Juggalos, too?"

"Lemme tell you somethin', young buck," Joker said as he lit a Black & Mild. "These neo-Nazis, KKK, Aryans, Proud Boys or whoever, can have a cross burnin' on their front porch! It's about that green paper. These 2020 Black Lives Matter mufuckas got it twisted. A white celeb calls 'em *nigger* one time, and they want their head on a spike, but we call each other niggaz all day. It's the same word either way."

"You got Crips *and* Bloods down here," A-Son said, showing everyone the list. "A lot of 'em."

The list read as follows:
Almighty Black P. Stones
Four Corner Hustlers
Black Guerilla Family
Double ll Set
Sex Money Murda
East Nashville Crips
Grape Street Watts Crips
Rollin 60s (Neighborhood)
DC Blacks
Outlaw Gangster Disciples
KUMI 415

Philadelphia Black Mafia
Almighty Vice Lords
Black Disciples
Bounty Hunter Bloods
Piru Street Boys
United Blood Nation
Du Roc Crips
Rollin 30s Crips
Venice Shoreline Crips
Gangster Disciples (Folk)
Hidden Valley Kings
Mickey Cobras (People)
Zoe Pound Gang

Joker was given his phone back when his men finished examining the gang lists.

"Them mufuckas got everything on the damned Internet," Ground War shook his head.

Fast Eddie went to retrieve Joker's car, a blue four-door Malibu rental he'd obtained from Enterprise car rental service in Nyack.

Eddie examined the undercarriage, sweeping it for any signs of explosives. Then he entered the interior and popped the trunk and the hood, where he performed the same sweep. Satisfied that all was safe, he started the car and drove it up to where Joker and the others stood waiting.

"Son," Ground War shook his head. "You said we a millionaire crew now, and you rollin' in this paper bag? Bullets can rip right through it like nothin'. You need a thousand-HP motor wit some armor on the shit."

Joker nodded. "I'll get it."

He was aware that War was not just talking about Khadafi but rather the retaliation they all knew would come from the Italian Mob. It was not a matter of if, but when.

"I have to head up north," Joker conveyed. "Let's ride."

They piled into the car and hit the road.

CHAPTER TWENTY

(*The Home of Angel Sanchez*Brooklyn, NY*Saturday 12:30 AM*)

"Whatchu doin' in my house, *Maricon!*" Angel screamed as Ghostman and Knarf kicked in the backdoor of her small house.

She lived across the street from Betsy Head Park on Saratoga Avenue in the Brownsville section of Brooklyn. She tried to run, but Ghostman quickly subdued the feisty Latina vixen and smacked her with the stock of his MK-7. She instantly realized that the gun had broken one of her front teeth and cut the inside of her upper lip.

"Be still, bitch!" Ghost growled.

She moaned in pain, blood running down her chin as she spat a piece of the tooth and blood into Ghostman's face.

"Ha, ha, that's what I'm talkin' bout," he smiled.

"*Go!*" Knarf ordered as a bullish red pit bull ran out from the rear of the house, barking and attacking Ghostman's right arm as it latched onto his black special ops tactical jacket with its iron jaw.

Ghostman slammed Angel against the wall, where she crumbled to the floor. Then he pulled out a long Rambo knife and nearly gutted the animal while Knarf helped. Ghostman personally carried Angel out of the house and placed her into the trunk of the waiting

Mitsubishi Garland. Knarf brought out the kid and laid him beside his unconscious mother.

"Toast it," Ghostman ordered Knark. "I'll deliver the package to the boss. Meanwhile, y'all know what to do next."

As the ruthless squadron of mercenaries firebombed Angel's home and continued their manhunt for Khadafi, Ghostman drove the gallant up to the Otisville ranch, not far from the warehouse. He called ahead to Meth Man Ace that he would be parked by the property and wanted privacy.

Many inside the EIE knew that Ghostman was a scary individual. He was a monster with an extremely dark side to him. Hence, the name Ghostman. Knarf had known that Ghostman was excited to do something evil to Angel, but tonight was not one of those nights to stand up for the innocent.

Ace waved Ghostman on through and went back inside to mind his own business.

"And you," he said to the young mother as he parked near the large aluminum and steel garage.

Angel, conscious now, had the look of fear and terror in her pretty eyes as Ghostman removed the duct tape from her ankles and hand, but not her mouth. He peeled off her gray boy shorts and saw the neatly trimmed brown fuzz above her vagina.

"That's what I want," Ghostman told her in an even, soothing tone. "You be sweet to me, and you and your son will live. Deal?"

She was shivering, scared, but nodded in desperate compliance with the rock-solid dark-skinned man sitting next to her. He got completely naked.

Thirty minutes later, after he'd had his way with her, he stepped out of the car. He was completely naked as the sweat dripped off his body. He put his clothes, guns, and other items on top of the car. She sat on the far end of the passenger seat, looking ravished and defeated.

"Angel," he said after he got dressed. "We'll murder your boy. Once more, gimme somethin'."

She shrugged.

"You either real loyal or real stupid," he said, grabbing her and retaping her wrists and legs. "In the trunk you go."

"Wait!" She stopped him. "The boatyard over in Coney Island. His grandfather owns a big boat and he sleeps there sometimes when he works on it."

Ghost put her back into the trunk and called in the info to his team.

———

(* The Warehouse* Otisville, NY* Saturday 2 AM*)

The two black vehicles were whisked through the front gates of the warehouse after the high-resolution security cameras were disabled. The cars were parked inside the main structure near the office, where Joker was waiting. Ghost arrived and popped open the trunk.

"The lil nigga and his bitch," Joker smiled that classic sinister smile of his. "You ain't got no drawers?"

"Joker!" she flinched at the sight of him. "Please, please let me and my son go," she begged.

Joker ignored her. "One of y'all get that nigga Khadafi on a burner."

Boo picked up the crying child and removed the duct tape from his mouth, which caused him to cry even louder.

"Got him, boss," Eddie said and handed Joker the encrypted burner phone. "Voice alteration is on, too," Eddie added. "Take that crying brat out back and blow his brains out."

Boo did as he was told, and seconds later, the suppressed sounds of gunfire, followed by silence, was heard. Boo came back inside, letting the door slam behind him.

"No!" Angel let out a gut-wrenching scream. "*He killed Junior*!

"Joker, you muthafuckin' coward!" Khadafi yelled into the telephone, cursing himself for underestimating the consequences of killing Big Al. "I'll hunt and kill everyone you love for this!"

"Her turn now," Joker stated coldheartedly.

"What happened to our vow to never hurt women and kids?" Khadafi attempted to negotiate. "All that fighting overseas never meant nothing to you?"

"Take her!" Joker barked the order to Boo and A-Son.

They snatched her up and pulled her while she thrashed and kicked on the way to the back. The familiar sound of a gun being fired was heard once again.

"She died with her eyes open, boss," A-Son reported loud enough for Khadafi to hear.

Joker Red emitted a dark, cynical laugh. "Before da night's over, we takin' it all! You hear that, Daf?"

Silence.

Joker took the phone, removed the battery, and smashed it into several pieces.

"Alright," Joker said. "He's gonna come out guns blazin', temperature hot."

The EIE army agreed.

"Somebody get Boo," Joker went to the warehouse office and sat behind his desk.

Moments later, Boo came in carrying Khadafi's son, who was alive and well but cold. Boo wrapped him in a blanket after slowly removing the duct tape from his little mouth. Angel was escorted in shortly after by Ghostman, who had found two large beach towels she used to cover herself with.

"Sit," Joker pointed to the office sofa. He retrieved bottles of water and Snapple iced tea from the refrigerator and passed them to her and the one-year-old boy. "Your man –"

"My son's father," she quickly corrected him.

"Khadafi," Joker stated. "Killed Big Al."

"Your brother," she nodded, wincing from the pain in her mouth from the assault.

Joker nodded in return. "We only want Khadafi, but unfortunately, others, like you, were caught in the crossfire. Hold on..."

Joker stepped out of the office to talk to Knarf.

"We got a few bodies in the trunk," Knarf told him. "We ain't wanna leave nothing laying around down there."

"You did right," Joker whispered. "Let me deal with her. In fact, y'all start choppin' 'em up and we'll get rid of them at the ranch house."

He returned to Angel. "Now I know you and your son got roughed up, but it took all my will not to exact my revenge upon y'all."

His men were all standing there.

"Why didn't you?" she asked.

Joker looked at her for several seconds before answering. "Because that ain't who we are. We are all ex-military vets who spent a lot of time defending women and kids, not murdering them."

"Well, Mr. military Vet," she stated with a cold glance at Ghostman.

"What?" Joker asked. She shook her head, afraid to admit that Ghostman raped her. He scared the wits out of her. "I just wanna go home," she said.

"That can't happen," Joker said to her, pulling out a laptop. "I'm sending you and your son to Puerto Rico with ten grand in your pocket... *after* we killed Khadafi."

"But he's my son's father," she pleaded.

"There's no negotiation," Joker told her firmly. "For right now, you will stay at my ranch. No phone, no computer. Once Khadafi is gone, you can leave. And you and your son will be taken care of for life. *Comprendé?*"

She agreed to the terms. She *had* to.

And that was that.

CHAPTER TWENTY-ONE

(*The Indian Sun Condo*Nyack, NY*)

Ace helped load the dismembered bodies of three men associated with Khadaf into a single fifty-five-gallon drum outside the meth lab. There were rocks and charcoal bricks with five gallons of kerosene already burning in it. Within just a few minutes, there would just be ashes left. Ace planned to scatter them in the Hudson River later during the cover of night.

Meanwhile, Boo, Bonecrusher, A-Son, Monk and Fast Eddie went home with Joker to the 15th-floor condominium he lived in. It was after 4:00 AM by the time they arrived there.

"Look here," Joker told his men. "I'm fuckin' exhausted. There's sofas, futons, and plenty more places to crash. The blankets and pillows are in the closet by the laundry. I got new Ts, socks and boxers in there, too. Use the bathrooms down that end, or you'll scare my wives half to death if they wake up and run into you. The kitchen is yours, aight? I'm out."

The ultra-king-sized bed had only Uzenna on it. She was soundly asleep and reminded him of a young Pocahontas the way her long red hair was pulled back in a single braid, accentuating her beautiful round face.

She wore one of his T-shirts and a pair of peach-colored satin Prada panties. She must have gotten overheated because the covers were down, and she slept with one knee kicked up as if she was ready to jump a hurdle. He saw a part of the labia on the left side, and his dick instantly grew hard at the sight of it.

He went to take a long hot shower. When he stepped out, she was sitting on the toilet, peeing with the grace and form of a cat. Joker loved it because she was so feminine at everything she did.

"What, man?" she smirked at him as she grabbed the toilet paper.

"Witcho girly ass," he grinned. "Wait a sec! Don't wipe."

She froze. "Huh? Why not?"

"Lemme lick it off."

She laughed.

"Ain't nuttin' wrong wit a lil peepee on it," he said as he sat on a cushioned bench across from the shower. "C'mere."

She flushed the toilet, washed her hands, and came to him. "Mmm, whatchu gonna do nasty man?"

He grabbed her ass and buried his face into her bald pussy, licking all the pee off it. She opened as wide as he needed her to, and she was on fire within seconds.

"Damn, I love that nasty ass shit you do," she moaned when he let her go.

He led her into the bedroom, and soon they were in one of the hottest, wettest, 69 sessions ever recorded. They groaned, moaned, grunted, licked, and sucked each other raw.

She could never take all of him down her throat, but she knew what he needed. She wrestled her dripping pussy away from his hungry mouth and got between his legs.

Using both her hands and mouth, she prepped him for her salacious tongue. She spat on his enormous dick and lubed it up real slick, so it was soaked from tip to balls. She swirled her tongue around the head and worked the rest of his giant stalk with her hands, caressing his balls with the love of a mother's hands on her baby's bottom.

She made the sweetest and sexiest whimpers on earth, loving his dick, adoring him with all she had.

"Tastes so good!" she gurgled.

He gasped as she massaged his perineum and circled a finger around his anus, sweeping his ball sack. "Ooohhhhhh, god...."

She sucked harder, deeper, like a goddess, like Cleopatra.

She felt how hard his balls became, and the big cockhead expanded as if it were a balloon. He suddenly slowed his breathing, relaxed his body, and allowed the cum to burst not just from his balls but from his entire body. He knew, as a man, how to enhance his orgasm.

She always tried her best to swallow all of his juice, but couldn't. Still, she tried because she truly loved the taste and scent of his creamy semen.

She curled up next to him after cleaning up the dripping mess off her chin and lips. They kissed themselves to sleep but not long afterward, she was reawakened by what she thought were the sounds of a baby in distress.

But it wasn't a baby; it was Joker. He had gone into the bathroom, turned the shower on, and closed the door. He was not only crying but screaming. Uzenna instantly felt absolutely horrible and scared for her man. She began to cry and banged on the door.

"Baby, lemme in!" she wailed. "Please open the door!"

Fast Eddie, the other EIE men, Iani, Coral, Romie, and Brittani came rushing in to see what was going on.

The other sister-wives were also awakened by the commotion and joined the others at the bathroom door.

Uzenna was beside herself with emotion. "What y'all standin' there for? Kick the door in or something!"

Monk shook his head. "I knew he was holdin' that shit in. I knew it."

"Nigga got me cryin' over the comrade now, son," A-Son said

with tears streaming down his face. "Fuck!" He didn't dare look at the others, knowing that they were also feeling Joker's grief.

Bonecrusher went up to the door and knocked on it. "Ayo, boss, we all out here cryin' for the loss of the homie Big Al...we here for you, man."

Seconds later, Joker emerged from the bathroom and hugged all his people.

All thirteen women were surprised to see Joker break down the way he did over the loss of his brother. He was usually a dragon-skinned individual, hard and ruthless. But the truth hides in the heart. Joker loved those he surrounded himself with. Each of his women now loved him more than ever.

———

(*The Indian Sun Condos*Nyack, NY*Saturday 7:00 PM*)

Later that evening, Joker awoke and tended to his hygiene in the master bathroom. Once he was dressed, he went out to the kitchen where the smell of steaks and gravy was heavy in the air. As the scent filled the room, his mouth watered.

Boo, Bonecrusher, Eddie, and Monk ate while A-Son washed dishes alongside Romie, the youngest Moses sister.

Joker observed how she was being flirtatious with A-Son, and jealous anger crept into his chest like acid reflux. Iani noticed the dangerous glint in his eyes and warned Uzenna.

"Romie," Uzenna called out to her. "Lemme holla."

Romie stopped and followed Uzenna into the bathroom. "Yeah?"

Uzenna slapped the shit out of her baby sister with no hesitation, stunning the hell out of her.

"What was that for!" she cried, holding her face.

"You playin' wit fire you stupid bitch!" Uzenna snapped, staring dead in her face. "You hee-heein' and carryin' on wit one of his fuckin men! Are you crazy?"

Romie opened her mouth to retort but thought better of it. Uzenna was furious.

"It's takin' everything in my power not to drag your dumb ass out onto the street right now and leave you there!"

Uzenna gave her an ice-cold killa stare and left it at that.

"This is a nice place y'all got, Red," A-Son complimented him.

"Yeah," Joker nodded as he ate. "And I worked hard for it, too, dig?"

A-Son nodded.

"And you see these thirteen women in here?" Joker asked him.

"Yeah, boss." A-Son squirmed a little.

"I worked hard for them, too," Joker added, staring him down. "They all my wives. I ain't gonna ever say it again to anyone in EIE or anywhere else."

Silence fell over the entire house because the threat was clear; the red line had been drawn. Uzenna went over to him and sat on his lap, and Romie sat down at the table to their right. They finished eating in awkward silence until Joker decided to lighten the mood.

"Ay, Britt, c'mere doll baby," Joker said to her.

"Uh-huh," Brittani answered as the other girls cleared the table.

"There's eight condos on every floor except the fifteenth through the twentieth, right?" he asked.

She knew the building the best because she had helped him research it when they were looking for luxury apartments to live in.

"Correct," she agreed. "The fifteenth through twentieth are larger and pricier. They only have four condos on each level."

"The other three on our floor still vacant?" he inquired.

"The pandemic been keepin' buyers out," Brittani informed him. "We're alone up here."

Joker thought it through as he smoked on a purple haze blunt.

"Let's buy the entire floor so we can have lockdown security up here."

Iani whistled. "Expensive."

"Get it done," he demanded. "We buy now, we buy low. After the vaccinations and restrictions are lifted, there'll be a real estate boom. We can sell, pay off loans, and make huge profits."

Fast Eddie had to interject. "Uh, boss...Ghostman texted you sayin' to call on a burner 9-1-1."

Uzenna hurried to go and retrieve a burner. She returned within a minute and Joker called Ghostman.

"It's over," Ghostman told him. "We got that nigga. Bad news is, we lost Fly and Lightfoot in the battle."

"*Fuck!*" Joker cursed. "What else, man?"

"We followed him out to Shaolin (Staten Island)," Ghostman continued. "He pulled up to some fancy multimillion-dollar crib we never heard of. I googled the shit, and it belongs to the mufuckin' Italians."

There was no more to be said. Khadafi had officially thrown them to the enemies. There would definitely be a war coming now. Uzenna put the burner phone in the microwave and turned it on for ten seconds. Sparks flew, destroying all of its critical components. She trashed the phone and heard Joker tell his men that Khadafi was dead.

Applause exploded in the room, but it was short lived once he told them that Lightfoot Jeff and Fly Williams were taken out.

"We'll take care of them nigga's families and kids," Joker said with a somber voice.

"Yu and Britt," Joker said. "Whatever y'all gotta do to get these other three condos, get it done."

"We on it," Uzenna promised.

"EIE HQ needs a new home," he said, bringing smiles to his men's faces. "My wives need to be here...cuz we all family."

"We need Fulton & Willoughby though," Eddie stated. "We not getting rid of it right?"

"The BK HQ is where we launch our entire lives from," Bonecrusher added.

Joker Red took a second to respond. "Y'all think I'm bein' paranoid but Ghost just said Daf pulled up on a Mafia mansion in Shaolin. "

"That means..." Eddie paused and shook his head. "Aw, shit. Whatever they thought they knew before, they definitely know now."

"Khadafi told them *everything*," Joker said, emphasizing it.

They all knew that meant a direct reference to the Villa murders.

"Okay," Joker sighed. "We have four funerals to do. Al, Lightfoot, Fly and even though he was foul in the end...I say we bury Khadafi, too."

That surprised the women but not the men. They remained neutral as they awaited their leader's instructions.

"If Ghost hasn't destroyed his body," Boo said aloud.

Joker stood up from the table. "We got work, comrades."

Uzenna stopped him. "Y'all always surprise me. To bury a man you went to war against says somethin' real special about all y'all."

Joker kissed her and rubbed her belly. "You're a better person than us, baby. We done some real dark shit together...and now to each other. All y'all girls are better than I'll ever be. And havin' these babies..."

She waited for him to finish, but he got emotional.

"Having these babies...?" she urged him on.

He shrugged as everyone looked on. "I can see a part of me that has only light in it...not darkness."

The men left not long after that, dressed in Kevlar vests, strapped to the teeth for a battle. Because now that Khadafi had sold them out, they faced an even deadlier enemy.

CHAPTER TWENTY-TWO

(*The Indian Sun Condos*Nyack, NY*Monday, 12:03*)

Several weeks later, following the funerals, Joker's company purchased the three condos on the 15th floor and moved in the rest of the sister wives, beginning with Leah, Valerie, Ashley, Melodie, Eden, Diane, Louise and Julia.

All of whom now lived under new identities.

The eight women swooned over their new condos. Four of them moved into one, and the remaining four moved into the other.

"We've structured it so y'all have joint ownership over both units," Joker informed them. "The loan forms that we have— TPP/EIE Inc. and myself— makes it a private asset of mine and the corporation. One I can write off as a business but still owe the lender on. Now, you are liable to make a mortgage payment of $1500 per month each, and once that's paid off, you'll own it—the deed of ownership transfers to you. For optics, pay me in a check. Of course, you know I'll 'give you' the $1500 under the table, but that's between us."

It made sense to them. It was a money-laundering scheme.

"It's so beautiful," Leah gushed as Joker checked out her provocative body in the all-white Gucci dress she wore.

Ashley hugged Joker. "We love it. Nobody ever kept their word with us."

"Them days are over," Joker said as he ran his hands over her slim waist and thick booty. "Damn, Ash, your ass makes me think of one thing."

She blushed. "What's that?"

"Lickety-split."

That made her smile. She was a cute grey-eyed brunette with a dancer's body. He loved the submissive and sexual nature of white girls. They were a lot more uninhibited during sex and the way their skin contrasted with his, had a sensuality about it all its own—especially when a big black dick was inside their wet, pink-white, pussies.

All eight of the women hugged and kissed him.

"Maybe we can get us some private sessions now," Louise commented.

"Damn, Lou!" Eden laughed.

"Just sayin'," Louise shrugged. "He's our husband, too."

Joker was flattered by all the attention. "No worries...three condos, I'll be in one each night. But remember, we a family and I love nothin' more than the marathon orgies we have under one roof."

He looked at Louise and liked her even more. There was a dark innocence about her, something like an impish child.

"Let's talk seriously," he said. "I know it's all love but no game. You all have me—no favorites. We gonna make beautiful babies."

Just the talk of making babies got the women horny.

"I can't wait," Valerie stated, feeling her pussy moisten. "You just don't know how bad we look forward to bein' mommies after the fucked up lives we lived."

Joker kissed her sensually. "I do know, baby. We gonna get there. Y'all have my word and just have faith in me."

Just then, Uzenna led the rest of the thirteen into the new condo.

"Hi, daddyo," Uzenna greeted him with a hug and a kiss.

He also leaned down and kissed her baby bump, making all the girls appreciate how tender he could be.

"They love the new condos," he told Uzenna.

"For over half a mill, they better!" Uzenna quipped. "Um, guess who here?"

"UPS?" he shrugged. "I ordered some shit."

"No," she shook her head. "Your entire crew. They down the hall checkin' out they new HQ."

"I'll see you goddesses later," he said and departed with Uzenna at his side as the two went home. "I been meanin' to show you somethin'."

She smiled mischievously. "You have?"

"Not that, horny ass," he stated humorously, slapping her growing ass. "Though our baby's makin' that ass fatter...next time, I'm gonna squirt warm chocolate in it and eat the ass and pussy for at least an hour okay?"

The erotic shit he said to her! "Hell yeah! It looks that good?"

"Damn right," he said as they went inside his section of the master bedroom walk-in closet and locked the door behind them. "No one comes in my closet. I had this floor safe constructed and concealed beneath this box safe as a decoy to the real stash.

He pointed to a secret switch on the top shelf where his shoes lined the shelves. He hit the switch, and the large safe slowly slid to the right. Inside, were pounds upon pounds of crystal meth and kilos of raw heroin.

"*Oh my fucking gosh, joker,*" she whispered. "Is that--?"

"Calm down," he told her.

"Bae," she frowned. "We LIVE here...and our baby."

"A hundred pounds of meth," he revealed. "Twenty keys of diesel from my Afghanistan connection."

"A *hundred* pounds of meth? *Afghanistan?*" she held her stomach and sat down.

"Baby," he dropped to his knees in front of her. "I know it's scary, but listen. The dope is a whole other story....EIE don't know shit about that. It's a big-time cash move for us, okay?"

She looked at all the narcotics. "Okay. I'm witchu. Now I know why you so confident about buyin' the whole floor of this luxury buildin'. But you also know we got heat on us. What if they get a warrant and bring the fuckin K-9s?"

"It's only a pitstop." He pulled her up, grabbing her waist and caressing her soft ass. "It'll take us over the top. I bet everything we had on this."

"You mean all our money?" she asked.

"Money, assets, everything."

She looked him in the eyes. "You're gambling our whole future?"

"And we gonna win big," he swore. "I won't letchu down. I need you to stand with me on this."

"I'll stand in fire with you."

He nodded and kissed her, really tongue kissed her until it heated up between them.

"You can't keep kissin' me like that without makin' love to me!" she panted. "Feel how wet it is."

He shook his head. "I better not."

But he did anyway. He put her on her back and peeled off the red panties she had on. He instantly smelled the musky scent of her pussy as he inched his face closer to it. Without hesitation, he went right in, tasting her dripping nectar.

She spread her legs wide open. "We about to be millionaires baby?"

"A millionaire Queen named Uzenna Jade Hodges," he said and went back to sucking on her clit.

She humped his face and massaged her breasts while he feasted on her salty-sweet mound. Her cream flowed onto his tongue and lips and he did his best to swallow each drop.

She screamed during her orgasm, and he licked her as clean as possible before he got up.

"What about you?" she asked, wiping the sweat off her forehead. "Ain't you gonna get blue balls or somethin'?"

"Naw," he said, turning his attention back to the safe. "You know I gotta take care of the white girls."

She laughed. "How much money is this stuff?"

"Ounces of meth is $2240," he replied. "So, a pound is about $35,840. The heroin cost me $300k, and I'm movin' it to the MS-13 here in New York for a million dollars, real clean. Add that to the $3.5 million we getting from the hundred pounds of meth."

She contained her excitement but blurted, "We'll be real millionaires!"

He smiled. "You feelin' it now, huh?"

She wiped a tear from her right eye. "I'm so excited I'm cryin' but nervous as a whore at confession."

"Don't be, cuz I'm a fuckin wolf, and this is what we do." He grabbed a duffel bag and stuffed it with ten pounds of meth. Then he took three more duffel bags and did the same exact thing with them. "See this? Four mufuckin' orders of ten each goin' out the door today to The Breed, Hells Angels, MS-13, and the Crips," he informed her. "In the wee hours, another ten will be distributed to our Wall Street and Dark Net clientele."

She helped him secure each bag. "Then the prison money..."

He nodded his head. "Hell yeah...that's a monster all by itself. We getting these bandz now. Didn't I tell you?"

She grinned as she watched him. "Sure did. I still can't believe prisoners are smokin' meth and K2 on paper comin' through the mail. It's astonishing."

He shut the floor safe and opened up the box safe. He counted out twenty neatly bundled stacks of $5,000 and placed them inside of a small silver attaché case. He then secured the safe, and they exited the closet.

By this time, the sister wives had returned to Joker's condo. He texted Ghostman and the other EIE members, summoning them over. When Ghostman, N9NE, Bonecrusher, Monk, Eddie, and Ground War were all present, Joker issued their orders.

"First, lemme say I'm proud of everyone's work and courage in our street wars," he complimented each of them, making eye contact. "We're officially a multimillion-dollar empire, and we need more front companies to legitimize our cash flow."

"Or bring IRS down on our heads," Ghostman mumbled.

Joker nodded. "That's right. IRS will shut us down. Anyways, right now, we gotta spend some money. Cuz Khadafi spilled the beans on the Villa thing, and we probably got hits out on us. That mansion he went into is owned by the Gotti family. Better known as the Gambino Crime Family."

"Victoria Gotti's a reality TV star," Iani educated them.

"True," Joker nodded slowly. "Big mouth bitch is all over social media, so of course, the major crime families know our name at this point. The Bonannos, the Luccheses in B-K, or the real boss of all bosses in Chicago, Big Frank Braga."

"Aight," Ghostman said. "So now what? That's all you gotta tell me."

"Armored cars, vans, and trucks," Joker revealed. "We trash the black fleet for an all-blue fleet. Cadillacs and Denali's with level five bullet and bomb proofing. Here's a 100k deposit to start. Cop ten of each and place the custom orders right at the dealer."

"Ten of each?" Ghostman looked surprised. "For twenty vehicles, $100k doesn't sound like a lot."

"It's just a deposit, " Joker reiterated. "Uzenna has the exact orders from online. She'll handle the financial end, paperwork, etcetera. Hey, Butterfly, arrange for them to be delivered to TPP as corporate purchases."

"Yep." She left to get ready.

"Bone and Monk," Joker said, nodding his head towards Ghostman. "Flank Ghostman. Heightened security protocol."

Minutes later, they exited with Uzenna.

"N9NE, War, Eddie," Joker continued. He pushed the four

duffel bags across the kitchen counter. "Four orders of ten pounds each. Instructions for delivery are in the text messages of these four burner phones. To assist y'all, call in all our street soldiers to move the EIE load. Then we need all hands on deck for the big weight deals with The Breed, Angels, MS-13 and Crips."

"Big boy game," Eddie whistled. "Forty pounds for now."

"Major distro," Joker agreed. "They'll all kill for lesser, so do each deal at the Otisville warehouse with one group at a time. Snipers, red dots on each target. Everyone should be in full tactical gear. Each deal is worth $358,400. They'll have a lotta cash and that means paranoia. Be on point."

CHAPTER TWENTY-THREE

(*The Indian Sun Condos*Nyack, NY*Tuesday Midnight*)

A winter storm had moved in, covering Nyack with a heavy coating of snow. Brittani, Uzenna, Iani, Romie and Coral were all inside the master bedroom counting the one million dollars-plus from the deals with the MS-13, Crips, Hells Angels, Breed and other contacts. Joker received a text that put a curious look on his face as he read it.

"I'll be back later," he said absentmindedly.

He bee-lined straight to the front door of the luxury condo and opened it.

"Valerie." He smiled and repeated her text: "*if you never had one that tasted like French vanilla, I'll be at your front door ready and willing.*"

"Mm-hmm. Hi, daddy," the twenty-three-year-old blond bombshell said, with a pinky finger in her mouth. "Is this a bad time to borrow my husband?"

She wore a long flowing lavender satin robe by Givenchy and had her long hair in an updo, which accentuated her long neck and showed off the red dragon tattoo that rested underneath her right ear.

Uzenna appeared and smiled. "Uh oh. She bad ain't she, daddy?"

He slowly nodded as Val reached down and removed her purple panties. She gave them to him, and he instantly sniffed them, taking in the wonderful French vanilla fragrance.

Uzenna came up behind him and reached into his sweatpants, grabbing hold of his enlarged monster cock. "You got an appointment with your other wives, daddyo."

He left and followed the curvy blond girl into the condo down the hall that she shared with Leah, Ashley and Eden. Valerie gave him an ecstasy pill and Viagra, and he swallowed both of them with a swig of Pepsi.

"Maria Sharapova," he whispered after they got naked on a makeshift bed of comforters, blankets and pillows she'd thrown in front of the big screen TV in the living room. "That's who you look like when she was younger."

Valerie smiled, got on top of him and gave him a "She's so hot."

He nodded, kissing her back. "I used to fantasize about how her panties would get caught up inside her sweaty ass crack and pussy crease when she played tennis."

Valerie looked into his eyes. "Your wild imagination. What else did you think?"

"Pullin' her panties down after a game...smellin' her hot white pussy...lickin' away the salty-sweetness...sixty-nining with her and watchin' her suck my big black dick with her pink mouth...until I cum all over her face."

She moved down and started to fellate him slowly with her small mouth and hands. "Keep telling me your fantasies. They make my pussy so wet! Who else do you want to fuck?"

"Llarisa Abreu on CBS CHANNEL 3 in Philly. She's the Black and Spanish meteorologist," he nearly gasped as Valerie dipped her head down low and licked under his balls. "She's so curvy and perfect. I'll suck her pretty lips, her neck, all on her titties, all up and down those golden thighs. And I know she has to have some pretty ass toes. I'll lick all over and in between each toe."

Valerie started masturbating her pussy with one hand, sucking more and more of his member into her mouth. Her free hand snaked up his legs and began massaging him.

"God, more, daddy! What else?"

He looked down at the Maria Sharapova lookalike. "I'll eat Llarisa's fat ass and pussy from the back. I know she got a beautiful pussy and a pretty little asshole! Ooohhhh, sh-shiiittt, whatchu doin'! Damn!"

She had his toes curling. He had to push her away because she was licking his asshole and had penetrated him fully with a thumb. He was on the critical end of busting an explosive walnut right in her mouth if he didn't stop her.

"Wicked ass little bitch!" he hissed at her.

He put her on her back and took off her high heels, tossing them onto the floor.

"My toes," she gave him a sultry look. "Pretty like Llarisa...or Maria Sharapova?"

"*Olivia Rodrigo,*" he whispered as he started slowly licking and sucking her pretty toes.

She loved that shit. "My fantasy all day when I look at you is to suck your monster cock, eat and finger your asshole, and have you cum in me so I can have your baby."

Her pussy got wetter and wetter as he made oral love to her feet with his dreamy green eyes closed. His dick was dripping with pre-ejaculation as it pulsated angrily the entire time.

"My toes taste and smell good?" she asked.

"Beautiful," he nodded as he kissed each toe.

He licked his way down to her bald, wet pussy and lapped up the liquid sugar pouring slowly out of her. How he loved white, pink juicy pussy just as much as his black girls! Valerie wasn't holding anything back either. She mashed that sweet young cunt into his face as she exploded into a quick orgasm.

"Fuck me," she begged.

He climbed on top of her tall supermodel body as he pressed his penis against her oozing opening. There was some resistance at first, but she took him.

He worked his mammoth shaft in and out of her pink hole. She kept asking for more, so he gave her all he had. She became more and more excited as he plunged deeper into her tight warmth.

"*Gimme that sweet white pussy!*" he moaned into her mouth, tonguing her down.

She licked and bit his neck, tasting his salty perspiration. "Keep fuckin' me! I love how deep you go!"

She melted and allowed every inch of that monster to enter her fully. She screamed in pleasure and grabbed onto his firm, sweaty, ass cheeks, as she free-felled into a series of orgasms.

She felt his body seize, his powerful cock hardened as he shot five huge spurts of semen deep down into her uterus and filled her entire vagina with his warm seed.

"Put that baby there, boy!" she whispered as her young pussy milked every drop of his juice.

"Oh god, yes mommie," he said, panting. "Take that hot cum... that's our baby right there."

"I love you so much," Valerie swore to him as they kissed and slowed down.

He looked over to his right and chuckled. Leah, Ashley and Eden all sat on the large leather sectional watching them with envy. Leah also held an iPhone, catching much of the heated lovemaking on video.

"Don't you fuckin' post that," Valerie told her, still breathless. Her juicy cunt was still squeezing his half-hard member.

"Y'all are so damn hot when you fuck," Eden purred, turned on.

"He's still hard inside me," Valerie informed her sisters. "My god, I can ride his pole all night!"

Eden was first to strip and lay down next to him when Valerie got up. Needless to say, Joker stayed and made love to all of the women until midmorning on Wednesday, the following day.

HITTAZ

"We've identified 295 gang members in 295 federal penitentiaries," Uzenna was saying to the twelve sister wives when Joker arrived into the TPP office. "We've sent them all meth, molly, acid and K2 paper. Enough for them to return $25k each."

"What's the total prison count now?" Joker wanted to know. "Including states."

"One thousand prisons, and twelve hundred ninety-five contacts inside," she proudly revealed. "None of them can be directly tied to TPP other than our legit businesses. The narco paper is always sent with no return addresses."

That was what he needed to hear.

"However," she went on. "Even when we switch PayPal, Venmo, and Cashapp accounts, it's still a digital fingerprint. The only logical way to do it without catching a case is for bank accounts to be opened in fictitious names."

"Fictitious," he repeated. "I like that word."

"Expensive and risky," Iani added. "What about when the victim of the ID theft discovers it?"

"Dead man's ID," he advised.

"Good idea," Britt said.

"Lemme work on law enforcement payoffs, too," Joker told them. The room went quiet when he said this. "Y'all thought we could get all this gwap and not have to bribe an IRS or FBI official?" Joker shook his head. "Welcome to the major league."

"I'll get on the dead man's IDs for now," Uzenna said, grabbing a burner phone and leaving the office.

Iani was sitting at the computer, and suddenly her face had a frown. She got up and ran past everyone, out of the office, and into the bathroom. Some of the other women followed her and saw her vomiting in the toilet.

"I think I'm pregnant," Iani told the girls.

The women squealed with excitement, and Uzenna smiled.

"I have a pregnancy test on the desk," Iani told Coral.

Coral retrieved it and brought it back to Iani. They waited for the results to confirm Lani's suspicions. Once it did, all thirteen women hugged and celebrated the positive result. Joker was very happy as well.

"Our family is getting bigger," he said as he embraced Iani. "Let's go out to dinner tonight to highlight this, y'all."

There was no shortage of happiness among the group at the news.

CHAPTER TWENTY-FOUR

(*7-Mile Beach*Negril, Jamaica*Two weeks later*)

Day after day the news of a new pregnancy came in, and each one was a brand new surprise. He knew he was the nucleus of the "family." His wives were regularly having sex—with the *hopes* of being impregnated by him—but for it to actually happen in such a short time was crazy.

But it had. All thirteen of his women were officially expecting a baby.

To celebrate the incredible feat, he took them on vacation to the beautiful island of Jamaica. They rented a multimillion-dollar beachfront château with its own private beach and yacht.

Joker couldn't be any prouder about what they were building. He watched all thirteen of his lovely women playing a game of volleyball, wearing the latest in fashionable bikinis from a variety of different designers such as Versace and Gucci.

He was lying on a nearby cushioned lounge chair, smiling as if he had won the lottery. He was actually laughing out loud and didn't realize it until Uzenna came over.

"Whatchu laughin' at?" she asked him.

He looked up at her through his Gucci shades. "I was laughin'?" he asked her.

"Uh huh," she nodded.

He pointed. "Thirteen badass young bitches, carryin' my babies. Most of 'em white girls. Asses all out on the beach here in Jamaica at this rich mansion...a yacht we can use. Millions of dollars bein' made. I mean, damn, ain't you laughin', mommie?"

She grinned. "Guess I am."

Most men had to wait many years to create a family with three or more kids, and here he was about to have thirteen within a year, with women he had saved and grown to love more than anything.

A day before leaving New York, Uzenna and Joker had made it official in the eyes of the law and got married at city hall by a magistrate. They decided not to tie the knot in the conventional manner because they were far from a conventional couple.

As a celebratory milestone, 7-Mile Beach was made in their honeymoon. The women were happy with the marriage, which couldn't have come at a more perfect time now that all of them had become pregnant at the same time. It was really a miracle.

"Baby, my soul is haunted by a lot of cold ass shit I did," he confessed to her as they lay out on the beach, looking up at the stars above. "I have heaven on earth. Thirteen beautiful women...a growin' drug empire...a powerful organization I'm boss of... millions of dollars...and I'm afraid most of losin' y'all and my babies."

She kissed him sweetly. "We a family, daddy. A real tight family. No one is like us in the world...except maybe the polygamists in Utah?"

"We are kinda like them, huh?" he said. "Without all that I'm a prophet bullshit."

She nodded. "Yeah. You kinda are a prophet... sent by the gangster gods. And we're all your concubines."

He laughed. "You funny."

Wearing an expensive Chanel thong bikini, she had one leg

draped across his, and her head rested on his chest. She comforted him as her right hand rubbed coconut oil all over his torso.

"Don't be feelin' nervous about us," she assured him. "You feelin' all these crazy nerves cuz you pregnant, too, babe."

He kissed her warmly. "You tryna fuck?"

She shook her head, no. "My womb hurt. I mean, it's sensitive in there. We can fool around, though. I can suck you and lemme swallow your cream."

He shrugged. "Nah, I'm cool."

"Where your mind be at sometimes?" she sucked her teeth, catching an attitude.

"Whatchu mean?"

She just let it go and lay her head back on his chest.

A moment later, he spoke on it. "I have alotta flashbacks."

She sighed. "You need to make an appointment with the psychology department at the VA Hospital because you have to keep ya head in the game, man."

"It's in the game."

She shook her head in disagreement. "I know you now. You want another war. You and your army do. Y'all need to be okay with the war bein' over...Amerikkka ain't Kandahar."

That sounded like judgment, and it irked him. "What the fuck does that mean?"

She sighed and chose her words carefully. "You can't wake up each day itchin' for another kill. In Kandahar, Syria, Iraq, and wherever they had you...your *orders* were to kill, bomb, and assassinate. Not stateside. Level out, baby. We gotchu. You got *thirteen* kids coming!"

He calmed down. He knew she had no idea how he truly felt, nor could she understand what was in the heads and hearts of the EIE Army.

"We are highly aware of all the dangers with the Mafia," she continued. "The good thing is that the feds ain't put y'all in cuffs. And the Mob? What if they let it go cuz y'all hurt 'em so bad?"

"I think that will be a grave mistake," he said. "Remember they never gave a fuck about y'all or killin' off your partners on them casino boats in Mississippi or Louisiana. The NYPD already fed them info on my crew...and now Khadafi's dumbass. Now what they tryna do is locate the 'missing strippers' from the Villa, so they can find the motive for the hit—especially when they see y'all pregnant...and you being married to me."

Uzenna was quiet.

"On a better note," he sighed and kissed her. "All the new armored SUV fleet are ready when we return home."

She looked up at him. "At least they're all blue, cuz me and you are havin' a baby boy!"

"A *boy?*" he repeated. "When'd you find that out?"

"Oops," she laughed as he pounced on top of her and tickled her sides. *"Ha-ha-ha-ha! Stop, Red, cuz you gonna make me pee myself!"*

He got off of her. "A boy? Wow."

"I'm sorry," she apologized. "It was all last minute. Before our wedding vows, I stop at by the doctor's office for a covid test."

"It's cool."

"So you bought Caddy SUVs. Am I getting one?"

He nodded. "Not a Caddy, but you are getting a custom-made Range Rover. A Queen's ride. Somethin' real slick."

She loved that idea. "Hmm. Any color I want?"

He nodded yes. "Course."

They walked back up the beach and up the stairs that led to the château, which sat overlooking the Caribbean. The other twelve girls had made it back already and were sitting around the straw-covered patio, drinking various drinks.

"I want y'all to order your own cars," he told them. "Use one dealership so we can get a wholesale price. Take the time to get your thoughts together on custom work, sound, TVs, etcetera. I'll order your armor."

Uzenna pulled her laptop out of the case and located a Range

Rover dealer in Westchester, New York. The girls gathered around her at the bar to see their options.

"The men got all-blue Denalis and Caddies," she told them. "We gonna get a fleet of Ranges."

"Range Rovers are boss," Coral mentioned. "I definitely wouldn't frown about havin' one."

"Cool. So, choose y'all own color," Uzenna shrugged. "We ain't gotta do like they do."

While they haggled over that color choices, Joker answered texts from Ghostman and Black N9NE. They were back in New York getting that Dark Web, street and prison narco paper money routed to Joker's new TPP accounts in the Cayman Islands. Joker checked the account balances via online encryption.

"Baby," he called Uzenna over.

She reviewed the latest numbers and smiled. "And here it comes."

"Didn't I say I got this?" he boasted.

She smiled. "I'm eatin' the crow, daddy."

"Britt," he said. "Have you been working on this hotel/money laundering thing of yours?"

She nodded, yes. "The idea is to purchase struggling hotels that buckled under the pressure of the pandemic, especially ones owned by foreigners who'd love to cut their losses. They'd sell above the table for an extremely low cash price, for say, $20,000, when the thing may be worth five times that. Under the table, we give them an extra suitcase filled with cash, a wink and a handshake. We hit the ground running and cook the books to make it look like the place is suddenly makin' money under new management."

"Okay," Joker nodded. "If y'all ever watched an episode of AMERIKKKAN GREED, those FBIs don't fuck around. So, if we build a hotel empire, we need meticulously cooked books, fake registration cards for phantom guests and receipts for cash payin' customers. The signatures must match the ones in the registration book. A lot has to go into a machine like that."

Britt nodded. "We'll need our own people. Not EIE soldiers, but maybe wives, girlfriends of the soldiers?"

Joker scowled at that. "Y'all think the soldiers y'all see in EIE are the only EIE soldiers I know? There are a lot more of us out there. "

Uzenna was curious about that. "How many more?"

"Life is a ride, baby," he told her. "Sit back and enjoy it."

She left it at that.

Valerie spoke up. "Well, now that you and Zen are legally married and all...what about the rest of us?"

Joker looked over at where she sat. "Whattaya mean, baby?"

Leah sat across from him. "We a family, right?"

He nodded.

"Well, we have our real names and new identities," Valerie told him, coming around to sit next to Leah. "The family dynamic is off...it's confusing."

Uzenna elaborated. "They...well, *we*, been thinkin', since we are a family, and all our kids are brothers and sisters...we should have the last name Hodges once and for all."

He smiled. These girls' minds were always moving, and he had to love that about them.

"I think that's a wonderful idea," he said, which pleased them. "However..."

The joy stalled with the word *however*.

"That'll mean going to court," he explained. "And filing petitions for name changes. Any jackass witta laptop can find out who and where you are after that because y'all gotta put an ad in the paper about ya legal name change."

Uzenna acknowledged that. "They know it. We also know the Mafia likely already knows who and where we are anyway. And we trust you to protect us."

He looked at each of them. "You already know."

Damn, he thought.

CHAPTER TWENTY-FIVE

(*The Paper Place*Nyack, NY*Wednesday 10:00 AM*)

Uzenna went with her sister wives to Rockland County City Court to file for and receive the legal name changes, which was routine everyday business at the courthouse.

The hard part was sitting around all morning until they were called into court to briefly explain the purpose for the name changes and to give anyone, the opportunity to refute the requested petitions. After hearing their reason, the request was eventually granted. Things were going smoothly for the girls, and they couldn't have been more grateful.

It wasn't until after the New Year that the brand-new fleet of bullet-proofed Range Rovers had been delivered to the parking lot of TPP. The women squealed with excitement when the two enormous car transports arrived and unloaded the luxury SUVs.

They fell instantly in love with their $100k custom trucks. The girls were so carried away that no one noticed the older lady standing nearby, studying them as each vehicle was driven off the two car carriers.

The old lady sauntered off in the stinging cold weather, down the street, to where the two white females sat in the warmth of their burgundy Ford Explorer. The old lady climbed into the backseat and took a fresh look at the 8-inch by 10-inch photos inside the file folder.

"Yep," the woman blurted out. "That's them."

NYPD detective Hanna Genovese to a moment to process what was said. "Whaddaya mean that's them? There are thirteen photos in that folder. Of those thirteen. How many of them did you see?"

"I told you already," the grey-haired old lady said. "They're *all* out there happy as a lark in the park."

Pope shot her partner a glance.

Hanna gave the older lady a twenty-dollar bill and let her out of the car.

Moments later, Genovese opened the passenger's side door. "What are we waitin' for? Let's go!"

The two detectives made their way inside the TPP's building. It had the look and feel of Staples or Office Max, only smaller. A great deal of care and thought about paper/office products had been put into the establishment. The detectives were impressed.

They noticed fairly quickly that there were at least a dozen customers inside the store's five aisles. Within seconds of them entering, they were approached by Diane Hodges.

"How may I help you?" Diane inquired cheerfully.

"Not yet," Sgt. Pope replied coolly, recognizing Diane right away from the file photo. "You sure look happy."

"We all got new cars from the owner today," Diane gushed.

"Generous," Genovese commented. "She must be nice."

"She's a he," Diane corrected her. "David Hodges—the best boss ever."

Pope nearly dropped her handheld shopping basket. "Oops."

Genovese noticed something else about Diane. "I hate to ask this, but..."

Diane laughed at her hesitation. "It's okay. Yes, I am pregnant, not fat! I love it. We all love it."

"*All?*" Genovese repeated.

Diane looked around before answering, knowing she was talking too much. "All of the women who work here are happily pregnant and due within two months of each other. Isn't that a miracle of God?"

Or Satan, Pope thought.

"Well, it sure is!" Pope said to her face. "How many of y'all are pregnant again?"

"Thirteen," Diane told her, suddenly feeling self-conscious. "Please excuse me."

Pope and Genovese were dumbfounded by what they'd just heard.

"Her nametag has an alias on it," Pope said in a whisper to Genovese. "But that's Diane Fredericks—one of our missing."

Pope and Genovese asked for the manager, and Uzenna came out of the office moments later.

"Ladies?" Uzenna greeted them. "How can I assist you?"

Pope made sure she spoke quietly so only Uzenna could hear her. "I am, Detective Pope and my partner, Genovese, is with NYPD. We've been lookin' for you girls."

"I'm sorry," Uzenna laughed. "Who are you lookin' for?"

"Uzenna Jade Moses aka Kellyann Gaines aka Uzenna Hodges," Pope rattled off her names. "Uzenna, listen to me. We're on your side."

Pope paused for several seconds.

"When you all filed for name changes, you were required by law to be fingerprinted," Pope explained. "Imagine our shock—"

"—our relief," Genovese added.

Pope nodded in agreement. "—at seeing your faces pop up in our CODIS system. We've been lookin' for the missing Villa dancers...and here you are."

"Well, go away," Uzenna told them. "What business do you have with us? We ain't missing, just livin'."

LOU GARDEN PRICE, SR

Genovese was getting upset with her attitude. "We know you stole identities from dead people. That's a crime."

Uzenna laughed cynically. "I thought you were on our side."

"We are," Genovese retorted.

"No one's arresting you," Pope assured her. "But we need you to come answer some questions about the Villa and your deceased employers."

"And Joker Red," Genovese mentioned. "And maybe about all this money you guys are swimming in up here. I'm sure the IRS would have some questions about that."

"Pipe it down, Gen," Pope warned her.

"Yeah, well," Uzenna stiffened. "Joker Red is my husband, so marital privilege is involved there. And I know I've got a right to an attorney as well as my right to remain silent. So, I don't *have to* say a goddamned thing to either one of you."

Pope nodded. "You are one hundred percent correct. Let's all pause. Breathe."

Seconds passed.

"Would you please accompany us to the Nyack Police Department to answer some questions about the Villa homicide investigation?" Pope asked cordially.

"Hey, Leah!" Uzenna called.

Leah appeared from the office with a telephone to her ear. "Yeah."

"Call Joker and tell him to send a lawyer to the Nyack Police Department," Uzenna stated calmly. "I'm going down there with two female NYPD detectives who have questions about the Villa homicides."

THE women came out of the office after hearing everything. Diane stood there as well, feeling stupid for running her mouth to the cops.

"Are you all okay?" Pope asked the women.

They nodded.

"Are you being forced into sex or anything you don't want to be doing?" The NYPD veteran detective questioned them, looking at their attire, their demeanor, and their baby bumps (for the few that could be seen).

"No!" Iani exclaimed. "Why would you think that? You see that we are happy, well-fed, clean, and we co-own this company." She shrugged to emphasize her point.

"Okay," Pope said to them. "I'll need to talk to all of you, so...."

Uzenna went to grab her coat and $10,000 Birkin bag.

Pope and Genovese waited by the front door.

Genovese quickly whispered, "I feel like we went from locating our sex trafficking victims to something weirder."

Pope nodded and put her thoughts out there. "You thinkin' this Joker Red has seduced these young girls into some sort of sex cult?"

Genovese blew out a whistle. "Like Warren Jeffs of the FLDS Fundamentalist Church of Jesus Christ of the Latter-Day Saints? Well, Hodges has a superior IQ. He can manipulate anyone or anybody, but I think something real strange is going on when *thirteen* women are happily pregnant at the same time. I mean, *look* at them!"

Pope was on the same page as her partner.

"Go see what she's doin'," Genovese said. "I have to call home."

Genovese stepped outside in the cold to make a phone call.

— —

(*The Chicago Mob*Chicago, Illinois*)

Big Frank Braga disconnected the call to his cellphone and lit up a Havana cigar. "Guess who that was?" he asked his younger brother.

Vincent "Vinnie/ The Butcher" Braga, was a mafia capo that had his own crew of robbers, extortionists, and killers, based primarily in the Windy City. But at any given moment, he could make one phone call and have an army of assassins mobilized and dispatched to take down a target. That's just how powerful the Chicago crime syndicate had become.

"Who?" Vinnie shrugged.

"My niece," Frank revealed. "The one on the payroll in New York."

Vinnie's thick eyebrows were curiously raised. "Ya kiddin'?"

Frank shook his head and puffed off the cigar.

"Ya not kiddin'?" Vinnie was all ears now. "What did she find out?"

"She found the fuckin' girls from the club," Frank told him.

"Fat Tony's girls?" he asked excitedly. "From da Brooklyn ting?"

"Yeah," Frank nodded. "It gets even better. The number one broad at Fat Tony's... Uzenna sometin'—she's married to da fucker wit the contract out on him."

"Joker Red." Vinnie filled in the blank. "The fuckin' spade."

"Turns out, there's a lot more than that," Frank said thoughtfully. "A hell of a lot more."

"Will you stop fuckin' wit me and explain everything?" Vinnie demanded impatiently.

"All thirteen of the girls have Joker's last name now," Frank told him. "Uzenna got married to him, and the rest got name changes to match."

"What the hell does that mean?"

"You ain't heard the half of it yet," Big Frank said, relighting his cigar. "They're all pregnant."

Vinnie's jaw nearly hit the floor. *"By him?* What is he, some Mandingo voodoo sex god? Did they form a sex cult or sometin'?"

"Fuhgeddaboudit," Big Frank waved it off. "We don't care. Sometin' way more sinister should have us worried. Get together your best men. Before the week is out, I want this Joker Red."

"What about the pregnant girls?"

"No." Big Frank shook his head. "Although they are my rightful property...just focus on getting Joker Red."

Vinnie tapped his fingers on the table. "Text me Hanna's

number...and anything else you want me to have on an encrypted phone."

Big Frank stood up to hug his brother. "That bastard and his army are savages...so be careful."

Vinnie nodded. "You know me. I'm not worried."

But even a cold-blooded Mafia killer like The Butcher knew it was smarter to worry than to be careless against a goon like Joker Red.

TO BE CONTINUED

OTHER BOOKS BY

Urban Aint Dead

Tales 4rm Da Dale

By **Elijah R. Freeman**

The Hottest Summer Ever

By **Elijah R. Freeman**

Despite The Odds

By **Juhnell Morgan**

The Swipe 1

By **Toola**

Good Girl Gone Rouge

By **Manny Black**

COMING SOON

From Urban Aint Dead

The Hottest Summer Ever 2
By **Elijah R. Freeman**

THE G-CODE
By **Elijah R. Freeman**

How To Publish A Book From Prison
By **Elijah R. Freeman**

Tales 4rm Da Dale 2
By **Elijah R. Freeman**

Hittaz 2
By **Lou Garden Price, Sr.**

The Swipe 2
By **Toola**

Good Girl Gone Rouge 2

BOOKS BY URBAN AINT DEAD'S C.E.O
Elijah R. Freeman

Triggadale 1, 2 & 3

Tales 4rm Da Dale

The Hottest Summer Ever

Murda Was The Case 1 & 2

Follow

Elijah R. Freeman

On Social Media

FB: Elijah R. Freeman

IG: @the_future_of_urban_fiction

Made in the USA
Columbia, SC
23 August 2024

41031495R00107